PAINTERS AND SCULPTORS BUILDING COOPERATIVE ZURICH

WORKING AND LIVING HISTORY AND PRESENCE OF STUDIO HOUSE WUHRSTRASSE 8/10

SCHEIDEGGER & SPIESS

1–16 73–88 137–152 245–260	ZARA PFEIFER	**DOCUMENTATION OF THE APARTMENTS AND STUDIOS JUNE 3–10, 2020**
174	GEORG AERNI	**PHOTOGRAPHS, 2020**
201	MARIETA CHIRULESCU STEPHAN JANITZKY VERENA KATHREIN & ARIANE MÜLLER ADRIANA LARA MANFRED PERNICE CHRISTIAN PHILIPP MÜLLER ERIK STEINBRECHER CONSTANTIN THUN GEORG WINTER	**INSERTS**

29	BRUNO MAURER	**THE STUDIO BUILDING AT WUHRSTRASSE AND ITS ARCHITECT**
96		**MEMBERS 1953–2021**
01	CAROLINE KESSER	**A SMALL UTOPIA MATERIALIZES**
21	STEFAN ZWEIFEL	**THE STUDIO AS MYTH AND VIBRANT PRESENT**
53	BURKHARD MELTZER	**LIVING AND WORKING— ON THE NORMALIZATION OF ARTISTIC WORK**
89	GABRIELLE SCHAAD	**"WUHRSTRASSE" AND ITS REACH—A CHRONICLE**
04	STEFAN BURGER	**A FRIENDLY PLACE**
29	ADAM JASPER	**IN ART WE TRUST**
37		**BIOGRAPHIES**

Series of pictures taken by Walter Binder, later founder of the Fotostiftung Schweiz, when he was working for the legendary modernist photographer, Hugo P. Herdeg, shortly before the latter's premature death. February/March 1953

THE STUDIO BUILDING AT WUHRSTRASSE AND ITS ARCHITECT

BRUNO MAURER

FIG. 1   Ernst Gisel, studio and house for Hans Aeschbach, Zumikon, 1947/48

FIG. 2   Ernst Gisel, studio and house for Paul Speck, Tegna, 1954/55

FIG. 3   Ernst Gisel, artist's house with studios in Ascona, project drawing, 1999/2000

The studio building at Wuhrstrasse in Zurich is the work of an important architect, and one of the most important works of the architect who built it. Ernst Gisel (*1922) ranks among the most influential protagonists of Swiss architecture in the second half of the 20th century.[1] His first public buildings already attracted international attention: the Parktheater in Grenchen (1953–1955) and two schoolhouses in Zurich, Letzi (1954–1956) and Auhof (1956–1958). By the time Frank Krayenbühl listed Ernst Gisel in Paul Nizon's *Zürcher Almanach* (1968),[2] he already considered the "rank of this architect" crystal clear. He identified him with the "architectural circle of the north" where, historically, "spatial-sculptural thinking dominates." He commented on Gisel's "expanded approach to functional architecture," which also "takes the needs felt by the user into account," thanks to his "empathetic approach to the specific and distinctive aspects of each architectural task. He has a knack for capturing the atmosphere suitable to a specific purpose, stimulating users and residents in this way."[3]

STUDIO BUILDINGS IN THE WORK OF ERNST GISEL

In Gisel's substantial oeuvre, which covers all genres, the studio building at Wuhrstrasse figures as the highlight within a larger group of works. The first project completed entirely on his own by the architect, then merely twenty-five years old, was the studio house of graphic artist Hans Aeschbach in Zumikon (1947/48). (FIG. 1) He also built three other studio houses in Zumikon at the same time as the Wuhrstrasse project (1953/54), followed immediately afterwards by the studio house for sculptor Paul Speck in Tegna, with walls of stone from the nearby Maggia River (1954/55). (FIG. 2) This genre spans Gisel's entire career down to one of his very last projects, a house of culture with studios at Via del Borgo, the main street of the former "artists' nest" commissioned by the community of Ascona (1999/2000, not built). (FIG. 3) The Aeschbach house was torn down in the year 2000, apparently without consulting historic heritage authorities. Its fate is most illuminating with a view to the Wuhrstrasse building, which is so well preserved and almost entirely in its original state after a full 70 years—a fact that can hardly be taken for granted. Indirectly, it is also a great compliment for the architect, who based his design on a concept that has evidently been capable of doing justice to the changing needs of exacting tenants.

One explanation for the quality of the building lies in Gisel's affinity with artists and the fine arts. Within his considerable circle of friends, they always played a more important role than, for instance, his professional colleagues. The very close relationship, for Gisel, between living and working, between architecture and art, is impressively manifest in his own townhouse at Römerhof in Zurich (duplex house Gisel/Estermann, 1996/97). The entry, covering the entire ground floor, was reception area, workplace, and art gallery combined. Much of his impressive private collection,[4] in which Wuhrstrasse artists are prominently represented, is exhibited here: one of Friedrich Kuhn's many palms stands next to the entrance; a bas-relief by Otto Müller is mounted on the wall behind the stairs. Gisel's work table is at the back of the hall and in the middle of the room a flat file storage cabinet, which, until very recently, had the latest project spread out on top of it.[5] (FIG. 4)

---

[1] See Bruno Maurer, Werner Oechslin, eds., *Ernst Gisel Architekt*, gta Verlag, Zurich, 1993, 2nd ed., 2010. The second edition of Ernst Gisel's monograph essentially comprises his entire oeuvre. The wish to honor Ernst Gisel's artistic work has been fulfilled in the new edition (Andreas Tönnesmann, "Der beharrliche Maler. Ernst Gisels Aquarelle," in Maurer, Oechslin, 2010, pp. 135–141).

[2] Frank Krayenbühl, "Ernst Gisel – Architekt," in *Zürcher Almanach*, Benziger Verlag, Zurich/Einsiedeln/Cologne, 1968, pp. 72–76. The Wuhrstrasse intimate Nizon also included portraits of the Wuhrstrasse artists Friedrich Kuhn and Silvio Mattioli in his *Almanach*.

[3] Ibid., pp. 74f.

[4] In connection with the planned publication of a book about Ernst Gisel's private collection, the Swiss Institute for Art Research (SIK-ISEA) started compiling an inventory. Unfortunately, the project came to a halt at the end of 2016 and the documents were handed over to the gta Archives of the ETH Zürich. The draft for the inventory includes a handwritten record of Ernst Gisel's spoken account.

[5] For a detailed description of the entrance, see Andreas Tönnesmann, "Der beharrliche Maler. Ernst Gisels Aquarelle," in Maurer, Oechslin, 2010, pp. 135–141, p. 135.

THE PAINTER AND HIS COLLECTION

Originally, Ernst Gisel aspired to be a painter. In 1940, the year he competed his apprenticeship as a draftsman, he participated in the Salon des Indépendants in Zurich. After attending the Kunstgewerbeschule in Zurich with Wilhelm Kienzle and Willy Guhl as well as auditing life drawing classes at the ETH, he made the decision to study architecture but cultivated a lifelong, varied interest in the fine arts and continued to make art himself, which he reserved for vacation studies. He devoted himself with great discipline to drawings and watercolors, during annual painting trips starting in 1960 to the south of France, Norway, and later, above all, Ascona, producing a substantial oeuvre over the years. (FIGS. 5+6) In 1990 Ernst Scheidegger Gallery presented a selection of his watercolors as well as ink and colored pencil drawings.[6] Kornfeld Gallery in Zurich held another solo exhibition in 2010, showcasing a representative selection of paintings, watercolors, and drawings.

A successful, versatile, and committed architect, Gisel wielded his influence to the benefit of his artist friends. He was a member of both the *Baukollegium* and the *Brunnenkommission* in Zurich (Board of Architects and the Fountain Committee) but above all he was able to call on artists, whose work he had followed for many years, to contribute to his public buildings. In the course of such collaboration, he built up friendships with other artists at home and abroad.[7] Sculptures, paintings, murals, tapestries, and, later, installations were not simply appendages, *Kunst am Bau* (art for buildings), but indispensable elements of the whole, which entered into dialogue with a building that was treated as a huge sculpture. This already comes to the fore in the first major public commission which catapulted Gisel into the spotlight of first-class Swiss architecture. Max Bill's 1937 sculpture, *Konstruktion*, occupied the center of the access courtyard to the Parktheater in Grenchen and it was, *nota bene*, the first purchase of Bill's work for public space, the field in which he would later become so successful. Gisel also repeatedly enlisted the help of artist friends from the Wuhrstrasse for a rapid succession of buildings in Switzerland and neighboring countries; indeed, three artists at once for the Letzi secondary school, his first public commission in Zurich. Otto Müller's stone sculpture on a brick pedestal dominates the large playground (FIG. 7); Silvio Mattioli created a stone fountain with benches for the smaller playground (FIG. 8); and Max Truninger's room-height mural *Musik*, painted directly onto the raw concrete in the music practice hall, presents the "spiritual center" of the complex.[8] (FIG. 9)

Other early examples include the two large murals *Sommer–Herbst. Winter–Frühling* (Summer–Fall. Winter–Spring) by Carlotta Stocker (1959) in the recess hall of the Auhof schoolhouse in Zurich-Schwamendingen (1956–1958).[9] The aura of Otto Müller's archaic *Grosser Kopf* (Large Head) radiates not only in the intimate courtyard of the youth hostel in Zurich (1963–1966), but also in two other versions installed years later in the open entrance hall of the Vaduz high school (1970–1973) and in the large courtyard of the Fellbach City Hall near Stuttgart (1982–1986). (FIG. 10) The Protestant church in Effretikon (1958–1961) represents a singular collaboration between architect and sculptor. The top of the architect's concrete, sculptural church tower, once hotly debated, resembles an abstract rooster, to which iron sculptor Silvio Mattioli responded with his agitated, crowing *Hahn* (Rooster). (FIG. 11) Unfortunately, the parishioners were not overly enthusiastic about it. After vociferous protest, it was removed and finally reinstalled in front of the Wasserkirche in Zurich.[10]

FIG. 4 Ernst Gisel, entrance hall of Gisel's home in Zurich, Ilgenstrasse 16, with works by sculptors Otto Müller and Hans Josephsohn, and painter Friedrich Kuhn

FIG. 5 Ernst Gisel, *Porquerolles*, pen-and-ink drawing, 1985

FIG. 6 Ernst Gisel, *Bornholm*, watercolor, 1962

The exhibition was accompanied by a limited edition catalogue: *Ernst Gisel Architekt:Aquarelle, Farbstiftzeichnungen, Federzeichnungen*, Verlag Ernst Scheidegger, Zurich, 1990.

Cf. for instance, the artistic concept of World Trade Center Zurich (1989–1995). See Marianne Karabelnik-Matta, "Zu den Kunstwerken," in *World Trade Center Zurich, Concept by Ernst Gisel*, Bruno Maurer, Zurich, 1995, pp. 35.

8 Truninger already contributed to the Recken schoolhouse in Thayngen (1950–1952). For a detailed account of the collaboration between Truninger and Gisel on the Letzi secondary school, see Benedikt Huber, "Sekundarschulhaus Letzi in Zürich-Albisrieden," in *Werk* 45 (1958), no. 5, pp. 151–159, 158f.

9 For a brief description and secondary literature, see https://www.mural.ch/index.php?kat_id=w& id2=1351 (last accessed April 23, 2021). On the friendship between Carlotta Stocker and Ernst Gisel and his family, see Peter Althaus, *Carlotta Stocker*, Verlag NZZ, Zurich, 1995, p. 53.

10 On the occasion of the fiftieth anniversary of the Protestant Church in Effretikon, the city of Zurich returned it to its original location on permanent loan. The event was covered in numerous newspapers, e.g., Adi Kälin (a.k.), "Der Mattioli-Hahn geht nach Hause," in *Neue Zürcher Zeitung*, April 27, 2011.

FIG. 7 Otto Müller, *Kuh mit Gestirnen*, stone relief on the large playground, Letzi schoolhouse, Zurich, 1956/57

FIG. 8 Stone fountain with seating and wall relief by sculptor Silvio Mattioli on the small playground, Letzi schoolhouse, 1957

FIG. 9 Max Truninger, *Musik*, wall relief in the music practice hall, Letzi schoolhouse, Zurich, 1957

FIG. 10 Otto Müller working on his *Grosser Kopf* for Fellbach town hall/D, c. 1985

HISTORICAL AND CONTEMPORARY PRECURSORS IN ZURICH

The beginnings of the Wuhrstrasse project are not well documented, but existing documents and oral testimony do allow for a rough reconstruction. Architect Ernst Gisel was definitely involved from the beginning, probably upon Otto Müller's recommendation. The two had met and become friends in military service, where Müller was the architect's sergeant. The three initiators Otto Müller, Max Truninger, and Otto Teucher were also able to count on the goodwill of politicians and the authorities. In 1949, the FDP politician Emil Landolt (center right) became Zurich's city president. as the successor of his deceased Social Democrat colleague Adolf Lüchinger (center left), thus ending the era of so-called Red Zurich (since 1928). However, this did not affect the city's promotion of the arts. The Wuhrstrasse project benefited from a venerable alliance between art and politics that had already been in place for decades. In Red Zurich, art for buildings and public spaces had become an important political objective.[11] However, the origins of the tradition go back even further.

During the First World War, many artists, having returned to their native Zurich from the art metropolises of Munich, Berlin, and Paris, had neither work nor commissions. Pressured in particular by the *Gesellschaft Schweizerischer Maler und Bildhauer GSMBA* (Association of Swiss Painters and Sculptors) and the *Werkbund*, the city began to hold competitions in 1916 for the embellishment of city-owned properties, public buildings, and buildings in the old town.[12] The preceding year, the City Council had already debated the issue of providing studios for artists.[13] Instead of the five studio buildings that had originally been planned, city architect Friedrich Fissler had two adjoining studio buildings erected in the Letten neighborhood (Rousseaustrasse 59/Spielweg 7), which were ready for occupancy by 1917.[14] (FIG. 12) The careful planning, which included inquiry into the needs of artists in Zurich and evaluating six city-owned properties, can be regarded as a blueprint for the Wuhrstrasse project. Once again, the initial impulse came from the artists themselves, who had already made several attempts to interest private investors in building studios for artists, though without success.[15]

Without another, almost simultaneous initiative, basically running parallel, it would not be possible to tell the story of Wuhrstrasse. On December 11, 1949, the *Baugenossenschaft für Künstler-Ateliers* (Building Cooperative for Artists' Studios) was founded with sculptor Bruno Püschel as president. The first general assembly and incorporation of the company took place on June 30, 1950. By this time, the location had already been found and the first phase implemented. Püschel and a few colleagues[16] had discovered an idyllically situated hamlet on Südstrasse in Zurich-Riesbach, between Nebelbach and Burghölzli-Rebberg. (FIG. 13) The historical buildings, some dating back to the early sixteenth century[17] —vintners' houses with adjoining barn and winery—belonged to the canton, which did not merely tolerate the "squatters" but actually supported them in building the first nine studios. The cooperative issued share certificates for which future users could pay by working on the construction.[18] Nine studios were ready for occupancy within six months after the founding general assembly. Before moving to Wuhrstrasse, Carlotta Stocker, one of the first tenants, lived there until March 1953 without interruption, except for a seven-month study grant in Paris.[19] Robert Zuberbühler and Friedrich Kuhn were also residents of both communities. The latter moved into a studio at Wuhrstrasse in 1959, but also frequented the Südstrasse, where his parents lived.[20]

When the Zurich City Council met on May 16, 1952, the Südstrasse studios, as visible and exemplary proof of the artists' own initiative, was among the arguments put forward in favor of the decision to finance the Wuhrstrasse cooperative by granting a mortgage on the property: "It is laudable that artists have recently made various attempts to take action and help themselves."[21]

11 Stadt Zürich, Amt für Städtebau, ed., *Baukultur in Zürich. Stadtzentrum, Altstadt/City*, Verlag NZZ, Zurich, 2008, p. 199. A publication initiated by Sigismund Righini impressively testifies to municipal support of the arts. See *Werke öffentlicher Kunst in Zürich. Neue Wandmalereien und Plastik*, Atlantis Verlag, Zurich, 1939.
12 See Bruno Maurer, "Das farbige Zürich," in *archithese*, vol. 25 (1995), no. 2, pp. 38f.
13 "Bau von Künstlerateliers im Letten," in *Zürcher Wochen-Chronik 1917*, pp. 63f.
14 Spiritus rector of these initiatives was Sigismund Righini, president of the GSMBA Section Zurich (from 1921, central president), member of the federal art commission from 1914 and founding member and vice president of the relief fund for Swiss fine artists.
15 "Bau von Künstlerateliers im Letten," in *Zürcher Wochen-Chronik 1917*, pp. 63f.
16 A.F. Vogel, "So lösten Zürcher Künstler ihr Atelier-Problem," in *Schweizer Illustrierte Zeitung*, 22.3.1950; excerpt preserved in the archive of the "Verein Ateliergemeinschaft Südstrasse 81."
17 The blue commemorative plaque on the building on Südstrasse 81 reads: "1508 Errichtung des Hausteils Nr. 81 als zweiraumtiefer Ständer über einem gemauerten hohen Weinkeller. Eine Scheune war wohl schon damals im Westen eingebaut. Zum Hof gehören das Waschhaus und das in Ständerbauweise angebaute Trottengebäude (Nr. 77)." [In 1508 a section of building no. 81 was built two rooms deep above a high walled wine cellar. By then, a barn had probably already been added to the west; with a wash house and adjoining winery in post-and-beam construction.]
18 A.F. Vogel (see note 16 above).
19 Peter Althaus (see note 9 above), p. 38.
20 Sikart encyclopedia entry: https://www.sikart.ch/KuenstlerInnen.aspx?id=4023405 (last accessed April 19, 2021).
21 "Auszug aus dem Protokolle des Stadtrates von Zürich vom 16. Mai 1952. 1002. Grundpfanddarlehen an die Baugenossenschaft Maler und Bildhauer," Stadtarchiv Zürich, see p. 53f. in this publication.

G. 11　　Ernst Gisel, Effretikon Protestant church, 1958–1961. Silvio Mattioli, *Hahn,* iron sculpture, 1960

G. 12　　Friedrich Fissler, studios and housing, ousseaustrasse 59/Spielweg 7, Zurich, 1917

G. 13　　Building Cooperative for Artists' Studi-, Südstrasse, Zurich, entrance façade with winery and rn, photographed in 2020

. 16　　Josef Schütz/Alfred Mürset (archi-:s), painter's studio at Brahmsstrasse, Heiligfeld Estate I, ich, 1947/48

PLANNING AND CONSTRUCTION HISTORY

Alfred Roth played a crucial role alongside the initiators and the admirably supportive authorities. Roth was Gisel's first employer (1942–1944) and also his mentor. In his office, Gisel was not only introduced to the tradition of modern architecture, but he also made the acquaintance of many of its protagonists. Roth, himself a talented painter,[22] gave the members of the cooperative valuable support by writing about the project in his function as editor of *Werk*, the leading art and architecture magazine at the time. (FIG. 14)

In the lead article of the December 1948 issue, he inquired "why, so to speak, nothing has been done in favor of our artists despite housing construction that has been booming for several years now thanks to public funding."[23] Roth then proceeded to outline the ways in which the public sector and private investors could support artists. He specifically pointed out that the Bohemian cliché of the artist no longer applies and instead described artists as modern painters and sculptors who are socially responsibile and work in "spick-and-span" studios. Roth came to the conclusion that artists are better served by being supplied with studios than through acquisitions of their work, "which always smacks of charity, especially when the works are mounted in some administrative office or simply put in storage." He concluded his fundmental considerations by presenting the ideal project for a painters' and sculptors' settlement, proposed by Ernst Gisel that same year "in collaboration with a group of young, interested painters and sculptors."[24] (FIG. 15)

The demographic development of Zurich was relevant for the public funding of studios. The rapidly accelerating growth of the city since 1943—on June 18, 1952, the 400,000th resident was registered in Zurich— necessitated the construction of numerous public facilities, above all schools and hospitals.[25] A political commitment was only logical to foster artistic contribution to these facilities. The fact that Landolt took office at the same time that the property was founded is significant. His tenancy in office ended in 1966, one year before the Le Corbusier Pavilion was inaugurated on Hornbachstrasse. Records attest to his generous collaboration both politically as city president and legally as a lawyer. The cantonal architect Heinrich Peter and the municipal architect (and painter) Albert Heinrich Steiner supported the cooperative.[26] The three painter's studios erected in the "Heiligfeld I" estate on Brahmsstrasse by architects Josef Schütz and Alfred Mürset are also indebted to Steiner's initiative. (FIG. 16) They were introduced in the same issue of *Werk* that covered Ernst Gisel's "Ideal Project for a Painters' and Sculptors' Settlement."[27]

In 1949, the year Baugenossenschaft Maler und Bildhauer was founded, Gisel was already commissioned to carry out a first project by Steiner that was to be located at Dufourstrasse in the Seefeld district.[28] (FIG. 17) The spatial layout largely coincides with his later design for Wuhrstrasse: sculptors' studios connected to a workshop on the ground floor with studios for painters on the second floor, accessed by a covered balcony. In the finished project, a residential five-story tower, added on to the street-facing front, housed the accompanying apartments, which Gisel had designed to be integrated into the complex. The top, attic story of the tower accommodated four smaller studios.

TYPOLOGY AND URBAN PLANNING

A distinctive feature of Ernst Gisel's work is his ability to translate complex programs into clear, comprehensible, and legible form. This is masterfully illustrated by one of his most famous works, the aforementioned high school in Vaduz. However, that skill first became manifest at Wuhrstrasse and the Grenchen Parktheater, built almost simultaneously. Several factors defined the studio project, such as the urban context, multiple functions (apartments, studios for

See Stanislaus von Moos, "Alfred Roth the 'New Architecture'/Alfred Roth und die ‹Neue Architektur›," in *Alfred Roth. Architect of Continuity/Architekt Kontinuität,* Waser Verlag, Zurich, 1985, pp. 9–33, 10f.
Alfred Roth, "Wer soll Künstlerateliers en?" in *Werk* 35 (1948), no. 12, pp. 369–374.
"Maler- und Bildhauersiedlung in Zü-," in ibid., pp. 375f.

25　　Sigmund Widmer, *Zürich. Eine Kulturgeschichte*, vol. 12, Artemis Verlag, Zurich/Munich, 1984, p. 51.
26　　Steiner's artistic estate is preserved in the Department of Prints and Drawings of the Zentralbibliothek, the public library in Zurich.
27　　*Werk* 35 (1948), no. 12, p. 375; *Schweizerische Bauzeitung SBZ*, vol. 67 (1949), no. 44, pp. 627–630.

28　　Only anecdotes survive regarding the subsequent change of location to Wuhrstrasse. The initiators did not like the property on Dufourstrasse and asked the city for a more suitable location (as kindly explained to me by Pietro Mattioli, March 3, 2021). See also Caroline Kesser's essay in this publication, pp. 101.

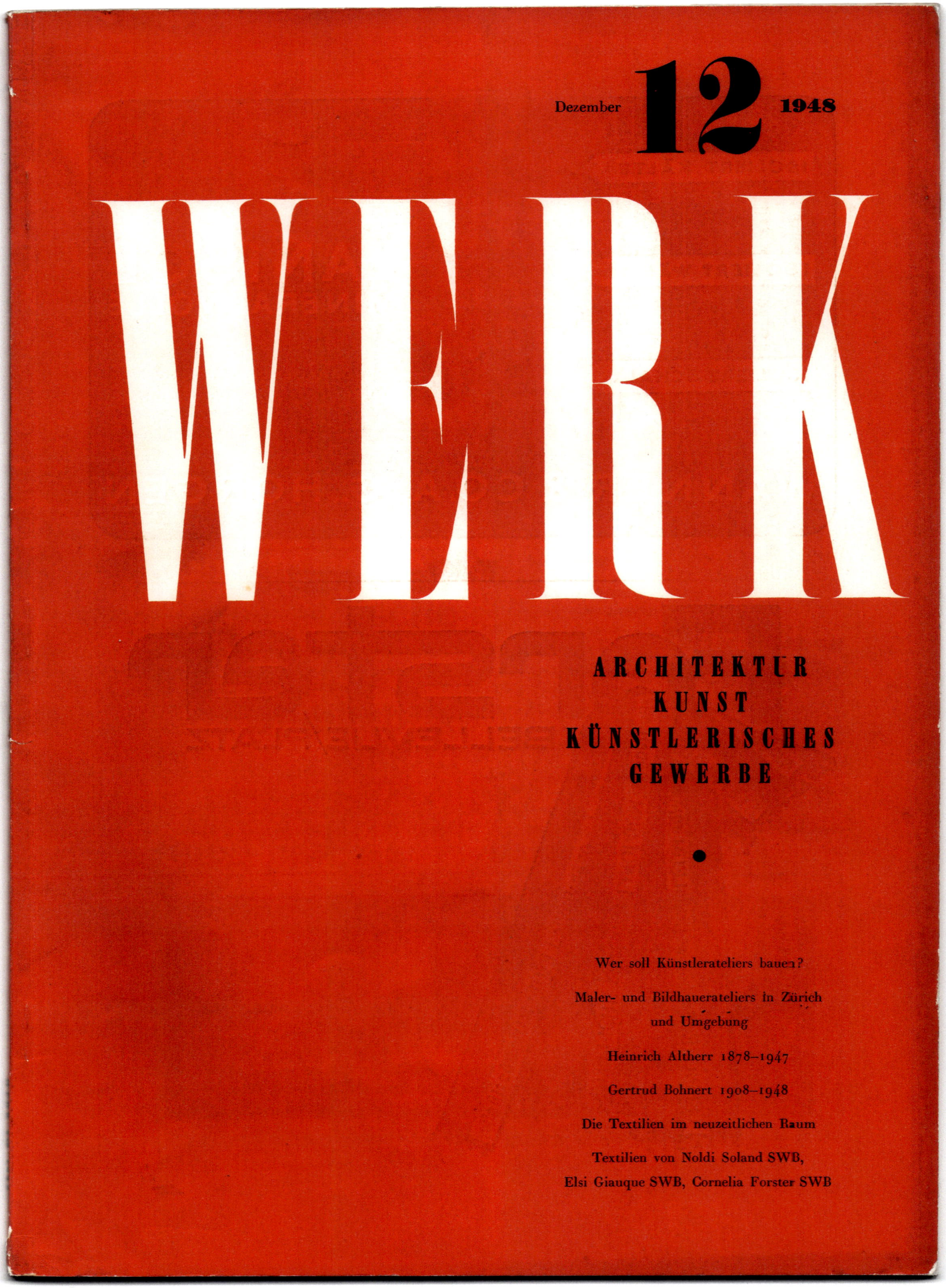

Dezember **12** 1948

WERK

ARCHITEKTUR
KUNST
KÜNSTLERISCHES
GEWERBE

•

Wer soll Künstlerateliers bauen?

Maler- und Bildhauerateliers in Zürich
und Umgebung

Heinrich Altherr 1878–1947

Gertrud Bohnert 1908–1948

Die Textilien im neuzeitlichen Raum

Textilien von Noldi Soland SWB,
Elsi Giauque SWB, Cornelia Forster SWB

3
4

FIG.14 *Werk,* vol. 35, no. 12, 1948 (themed
issue on studio housing in Zurich and environs)

WERK

Dezember 1948   35. Jahrgang   Heft 12

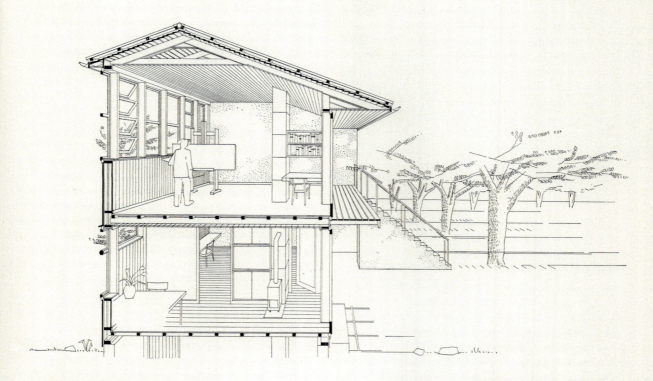

Maleratelier aus der projektierten Künstlersiedlung bei Zürich. Ernst Gisel SWB, Architekt, Zürich / Atelier de peintre, dans une cité d'artistes projetée pour les environs de Zurich / Painter's studio in a projected artists' settlement near Zurich

Wer soll Künstlerateliers bauen?

Von Alfred Roth

Die Zahl der den Malern und Bildhauern in unseren Schweizer Städten zur Verfügung stehenden und eigens zu diesem Zwecke errichteten Ateliers ist bekanntlich äußerst gering, so daß es vor allem für den jungen, noch nicht arrivierten Künstler, der es sich aus finanziellen Gründen nicht leisten kann, etwas Eigenes zu errichten, außerordentlich schwierig ist, einen geeigneten Arbeitsraum, wenn immer möglich mit Wohngelegenheit, zu erschwinglichem Preise mieten zu können. Es dürfte daher angebracht sein, dieses Problem einmal etwas näher zu betrachten und zu fragen, woher es kommt, daß trotz der seit einigen Jahren auf Hochtouren laufenden, den öffentlichen Fiskus beanspruchenden Wohnbautätigkeit sozusagen nichts zu Gunsten unserer Künstler geschehen ist.

Es soll daher im Folgenden versucht werden, weniger die spezifisch architektonische Frage aufzuwerfen, als einige Klarheit in die mehr allgemeinen äußeren Umstände zu bringen, wobei wir uns voll bewußt sind, daß es hier um ein komplizierteres Problem geht, als man auf den ersten Blick annimmt. Die in Gesprächen mit Künstlern, Architekten, Vertretern von Behörden gemachten Feststellungen sollen dazu benützt werden,

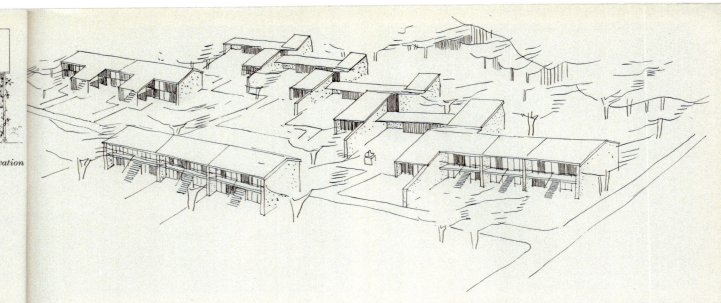

Gesamtansicht der Künstlersiedlung von Südosten / Vue d'ensemble de la cité d'artistes, prise de sud-est / The artists' settlement seen from south east

Maler- und Bildhauersiedlung in Zürich

Projekt 1948, Ernst Gisel SWB, Architekt Zürich,

Es handelt sich um ein Idealprojekt, das der Architekt in Zusammenarbeit mit einer Gruppe jüngerer interessierter Maler und Bildhauer ausgearbeitet und der zürcherischen Behörde zur Erwägung einer eventuellen finanziellen Beihilfe eingereicht hat.

Das Ganze hat eine zu diesem Zwecke noch zu bildende «Künstler-Genossenschaft» zur Grundlage und ist ein Vorschlag, auf den schon im Hauptaufsatz dieses Heftes als besonders interessant und real hingewiesen wird. Es wird ein Gelände in der Nähe der Stadt angenommen, das, wie dem Berichte zu entnehmen, in «Baurecht» übernommen gedacht ist, um die großen Kosten des käuflichen Erwerbes zu umgehen.

Der Projektverfasser geht von der richtigen Vorstellung aus, daß einer solchen Siedlungseinheit eine möglichst lebendige Gliederung zu verleihen und verschiedenen Ansprüchen bezüglich Größe und Art der einzelnen Ateliers gerecht zu werden ist. Deshalb werden mindestens vier verschiedene Typen vorgeschlagen, die grundsätzlich alle mit Wohngelegenheit versehen sind. Die Bildhauerateliers liegen zu ebener Erde, während die Malerateliers meist über dem Wohnteil im Obergeschoß angeordnet sind. Eine enge Verbindung von Wohnteil und Garten wird überall angestrebt und ebenso eine möglichst ansprechende innenräumliche Gestaltung.

In bautechnischer Hinsicht wird der Vorschlag gemacht, solid, aber möglichst leicht und billig zu bauen, unter Verwendung eines einheitlichen Konstruktionssystems und standardisierter Bauelemente. Unter Voraussetzung einer angemessenen Subventionierung wird mit Monatsmieten von Fr. 75.— bis Fr. 150.— je nach Art und Größe des Ateliers gerechnet.

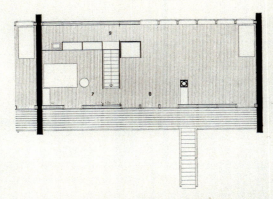

Obergeschoß, Maleratelier, Typ A, 1:200 / Etage, atelier de peintre, type A / Upper floor, painter's studio, type A

1 Eingang
2 Eßküche
3 Kellerabgang
4 Wohnraum
5 Kinder
6 Sitzplatz
7 Eltern
8 Maleratelier
9 Abstellraum
10 Geräte

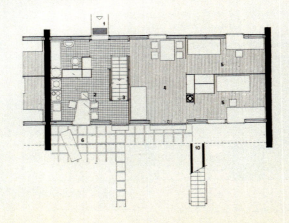

Erdgeschoß, Typ A, 1:200 / Rez-de-chaussée, type A / Ground-floor, type A

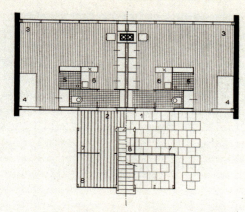

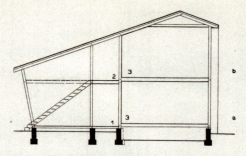

Ober- und Erdgeschoß, Typ B (Schüler-Atelier), 1:200 / Etage et rez-de-chaussée, type B (ateliers d'élèves) / Upper and ground floors, type B (apprentices studios)

Querschnitt durch Typ B 1:200 / Coupe du type B / Section through the B type

1, 2 Eingang
3 Maleratelier
4 Schlafnische
5 Dusche
6 Kochnische
7 Vorplatz
8 Schopf

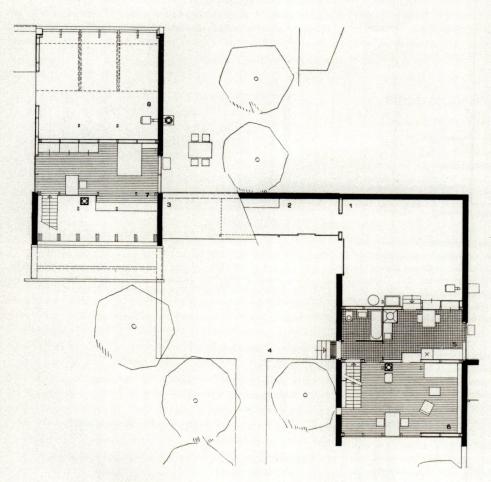

Typ C, großes Bildhaueratelier mit Wohnung 1:200, links Obergeschoß, rechts Erdgeschoß / Type C, grand atelier de sculpteur avec appartement; à gauche l'étage, à droite le rez-de-chaussée / Type C, large sculptor's studio with flat; upper story at left, ground floor at right

1 Bildhaueratelier
2 Schopf
3 Gartensitzplatz
4 Arbeitsplatz im Freien
5 Eßküche
6 Wohnraum
7 Elternschlafzimmer (souspente)
8 Luftraum Atelier

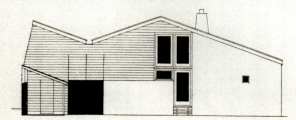

Westfassade mit großem Tor zum Atelier / Façade ouest avec grande porte de l'atelier / West elevation with large studio door

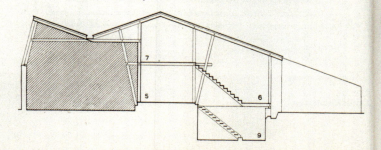

Längsschnitt durch Atelier und Wohnteil 1:200 / Coupe longitudinale de l'atelier et de l'appartement / Longitudinal section through the studio and the flat

FIG. 18　　Ernst Gisel, three studio buildings in Zumikon, 1953/54

FIG. 19　　Werkbund Estate Neubühl, studio building "Type N," Zurich-Wollishofen, 1929–1932

FIG. 20　　Ernst Schindler, Dolderstrasse studio building, Zurich 1939/40, photographed in 2021

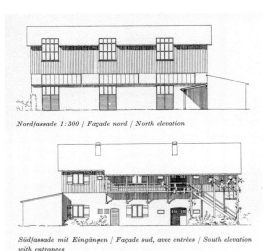

FIG. 21　　Heinrich Bräm, studio for sculptors and painters in Zurich (project, 1946), *Werk*, vol. 35, no. 12, 1948

painters, workshops for sculptors), and restrictions regarding space and budget. The singularity of Gisel's design becomes apparent upon looking for possible models or predecessors. The architectural task of building an "artists' house" certainly has a time-honored history.[29] Other noteworthy examples can be found in Zurich and environs in addition to those mentioned above, such as Arnold Böcklin's and Hermann Hallers's freestanding studios as well as the combined studios and homes of Max Bill and Gotthard Schuh. In fact, not a few artists of means built studio homes of their own or had them built in correspondingly affluent communities on the outskirts of Zurich. In Gisel's oeuvre, three such studio homes on Küsnachterstrasse in Zumikon are suburban counterparts to the Wuhrstrasse studios, built at practically the same time. Gisel and his family moved into one of these and another became the home of painter Walter Sautter, who had originally been interested in a studio at Wuhrstrasse. (FIG. 18)

Nonetheless, there are few models for the architectural task of organizing a considerable number of studios and apartments within a functional whole. Gisel was no doubt familiar with Fissler's two studio buildings in Letten, but they had little to contribute to questions of typology, design, and style at Wuhrstrasse.[30] Gisel certainly knew about the studios in the Neubühl settlement in Zurich-Wollishofen (1932) and had played football (soccer) on the large meadow in front of it as a boy. "Type N" comprises a slightly staggered row of three buildings, each with two studios and corresponding apartments above them.[31] (FIG. 19) Ernst Schindler's apartment and studio building in Zurich-Hottingen (1939–40) shows an entirely different solution. The four studios form a single wing at the corner of the angular residential building. (FIG. 20) Hans Finsler, who shot some of the most beautiful photographs of the Wuhrstrasse cooperative, worked in one of those studios. Unbuilt projects might also have served as a reference, such as Heinrich Bräm's earlier project for a studio building at Dufourstrasse in Zurich, in which the proposed arrangement of sculptors' and painters' studios (the latter with gallery access) was analogus to Wuhrstrasse. In *Werk*, no. 12, 1948, a themed issue on the studio, the article on this project precedes Gisel's "Ideal Project."[32] (FIG. 21) Gisel may also have studied the design of the "Ateliers d'Art Réunis" in La Chaux-de-Fonds (1910) in the first volume of Le Corbusier's and Pierre Jeanneret's complete works. There, the studios are centered around a "salle du cours" with a pyramid-shaped roof. (FIG. 22) Despite all the common ground, a decisive distinction remains: the client of the studio building was a building cooperative with entirely pragmatic goals; thus anything but a "school" or an artists' collective committed to a "unité de doctrine." Gisel's proposal clearly takes this into account. The sense of community is not celebrated in striking symbolic form. The eight studios for painters and sculptors are horizontally lined up in a row on two floors. The eight apartments, stacked on four floors, are topped off by four additional, smaller studios. There are no communal facilities. Encounters are possible—especially in the courtyard—but not forced. The project does not reflect Gisel's understanding of his work as an architect, as revealed in comparison with the studio that he built for himself and his staff at Streulistrasse in Zurich-Hottingen (1972/73). This "Blaue Atelier" has the character of a workshop and shares several features of the Wuhrstrasse building: the inner courtyard, the sawtooth roof pointing north, and the intimate entry hidden behind a high wall. (FIG. 23)

Looking back one can observe that, in the course of all those years, social life at Wuhrstrasse did not differ fundamentally from other cooperative settlements. Despite at times divergent artistic approaches, these were no sources of conflict but rather the contingencies of everyday life. Moreover, the complex was not a closed entity; it was always part of the neighborhood. Wuhrstrasse is on one of Zurich's beautiful residential streets.[33] Late-historicist perimeter block buildings and apartment houses of exposed brick dominate, in some cases with low workshop buildings in the inner courtyards. Having adopted these features, the residential tower and studio wing fit quite naturally into the street as a whole.

29　　Cf. Eduard Hüttinger, ed., *Künstlerhäuser von der Renaissance bis zur Gegenwart*, Waser/Prestel, Zurich/Munich, 1985; *Kunst+Architektur in der Schweiz k+a*, 66. Jg. (2015), no. 1 (dossier "Künstlerhäuser und Ateliers").

30　　Short description in the *INSA Inventar der neueren Schweizer Architektur 1850–1920*, vol. 10, p. 392: "Heimatstilbau unter Mansardenwalmdach über T-förmigem Grundriss; Jugendstildekor. Grosse Fensterflächen. Arbeitsort prominenter Schweizer Künstler." [Traditional *Heimatstil* building with hipped roof above a T-shaped ground plan; Art Nouveau decor. Large windows. Workplace of prominent Swiss artists.]

31　　See Ueli Marbach, Arthur Rüegg, *Werkbundsiedlung Neubühl in Zürich-Wollishofen 1928–1932. Ihre Entstehung und Erneuerung*, gta Verlag, Zurich, 1990, pp. 85–87.

32　　"Bildhauer- und Malerateliers in Zürich," in *Werk* 35 (1948), no. 12, p. 78.

33　　INSA, vol. 10, pp. 432f.

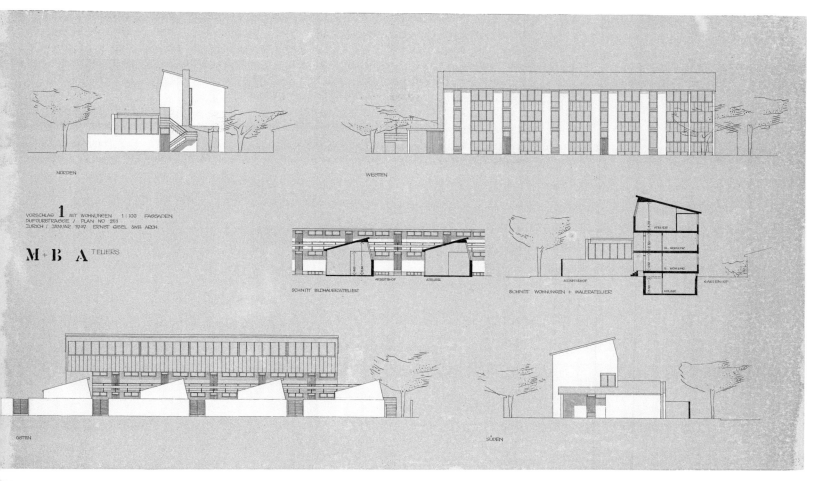
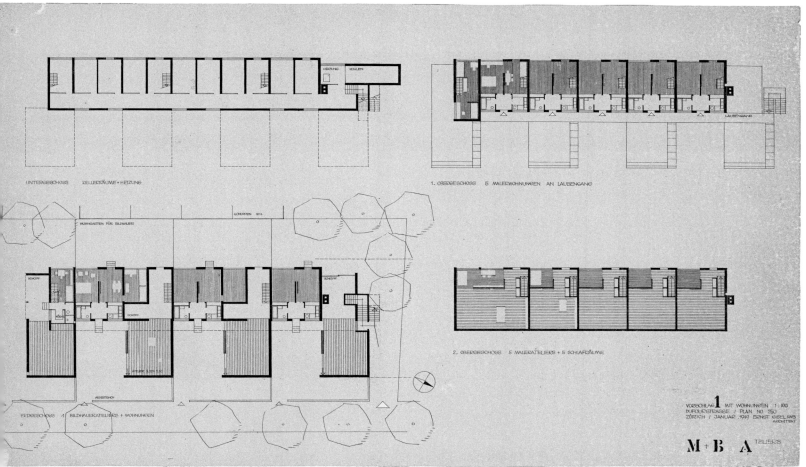

.17 Ernst Gisel, *Projekt Dufourstrasse, Vorschlag 1*, architectural drafting paper, Plan No. 251, 1949

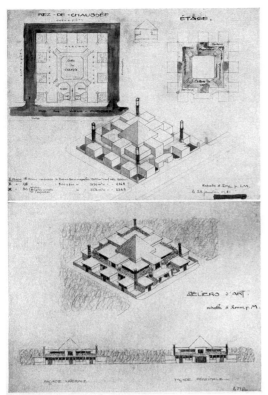

FIG. 22   Charles-Edouard Jeanneret, Ateliers d'Art Réunis, 1910 (Le Corbusier et Pierre Jeanneret, *Œuvre complète 1910–1929*, Zurich, 1930)

FIG. 23   Ernst Gisel, *Blaues Atelier,* behind the residential building of 1958–1960 at Hegibachstrasse, Zurich, 1970–1973

There is little that singles out the particular function of the building although the curiosity of passersby may be piqued by Otto Müller's bas-relief on the street-façade or the sawtooth roof in gray Eternit seen beyond the high surrounding wall. The building conforms, as if deliberately, to the bourgeois residential neighborhood, and seems to bolster the image of the new artist advanced by Alfred Roth in his above-mentioned article for *Werk*.

Many artists' buildings have been deprived of their original function and converted into museums or monuments, not infrequently fostering a genius cult. The studio building of the Painters and Sculptors Building Cooperative Zurich will not suffer a similar fate, thanks to the sustainable architectural concept that has ensured its survival as a vibrant, living organism.

This essay is an extended and updated version of my contribution "Das Atelierhaus und sein Architekt" in the brochure on the occasion of the 50th anniversary of the studio building Wuhrstrasse, in: Pietro Mattioli (ed.), *50 Jahre Baugenossenschaft Maler und Bildhauer Wuhrstrasse 8/10,* Eigenverlag, Zürich 2003, pp. 6–13.

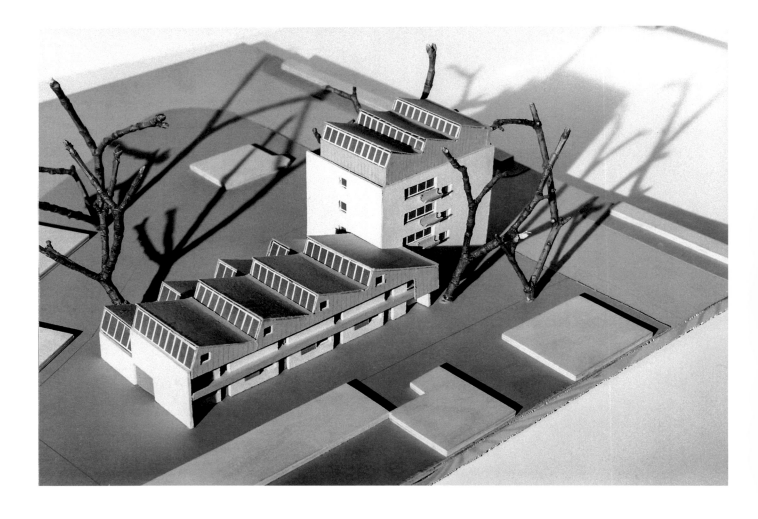

Ernst Gisel, model of *Atelierhaus Wuhrstrasse* (residential building with unrealized balconies and loggias), c. 1951

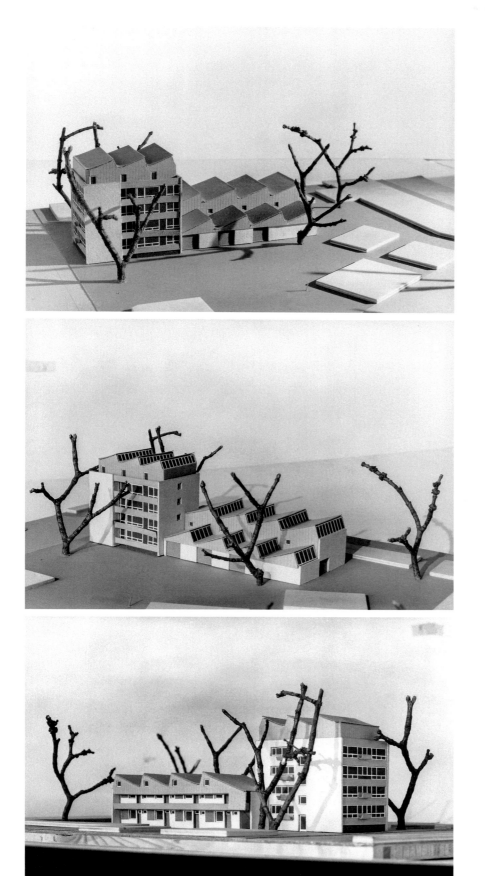

Ernst Gisel, *Atelierhaus Wuhrstrasse, Plan No. 1046*,
longitudinal section 1:50, August 6, 1952

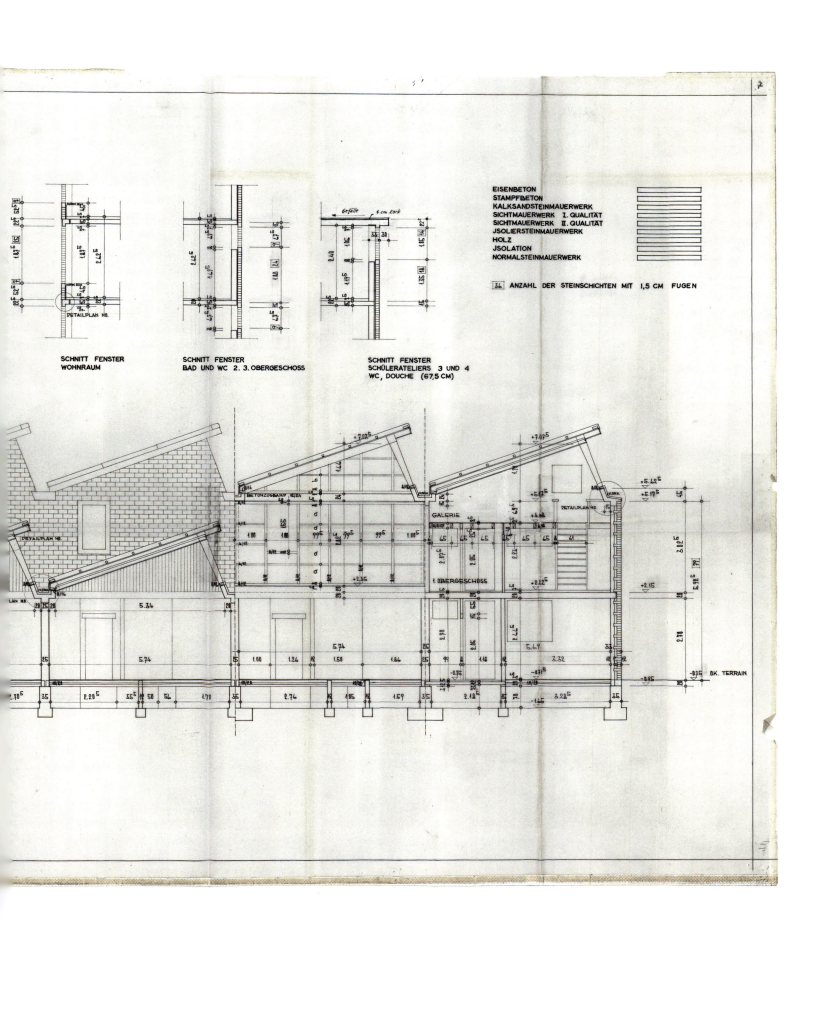

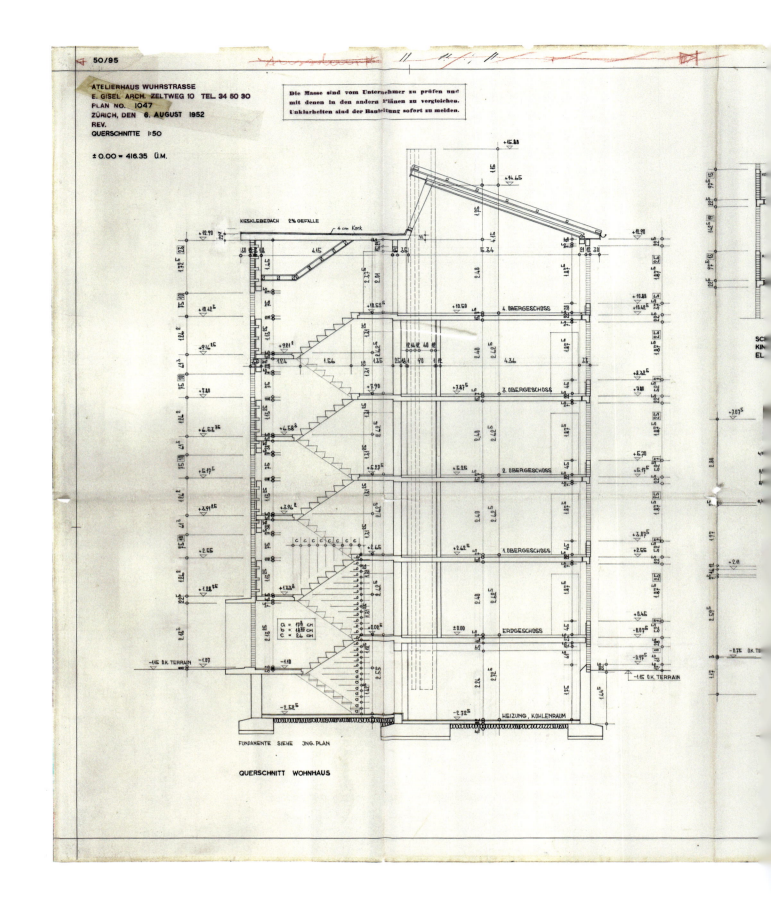

Ernst Gisel, *Atelierhaus Wuhrstrasse, Plan No. 1047*, cross section 1:50, August 6, 1952

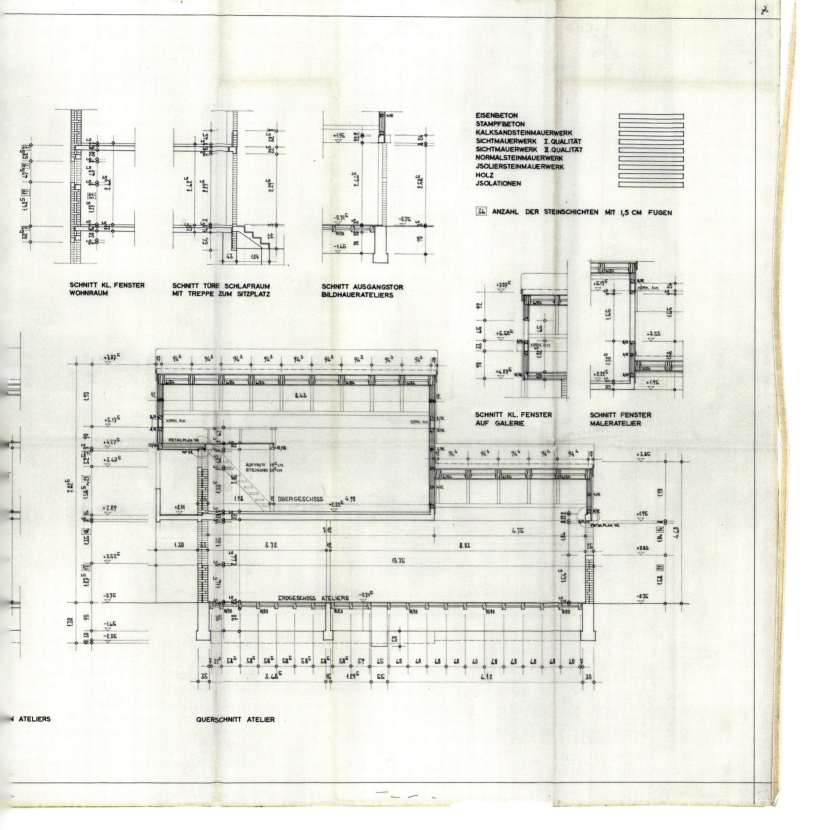

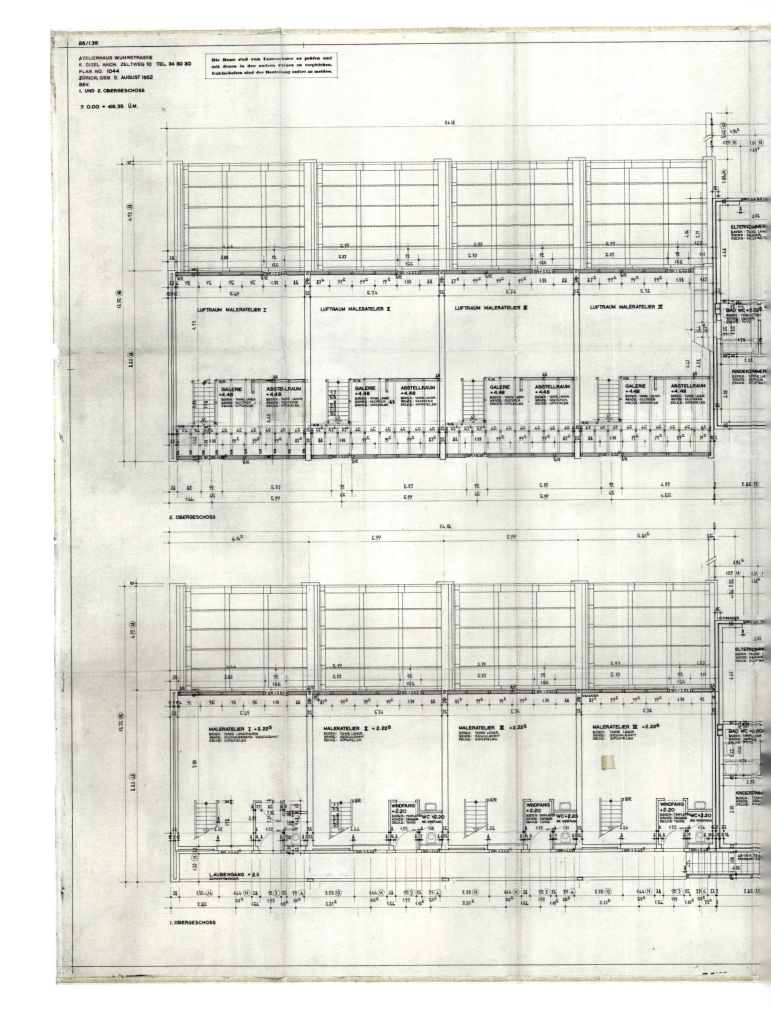

Ernst Gisel, *Atelierhaus Wuhrstrasse, Plan No. 1044*, 1st and 2nd floors, August 11, 1952

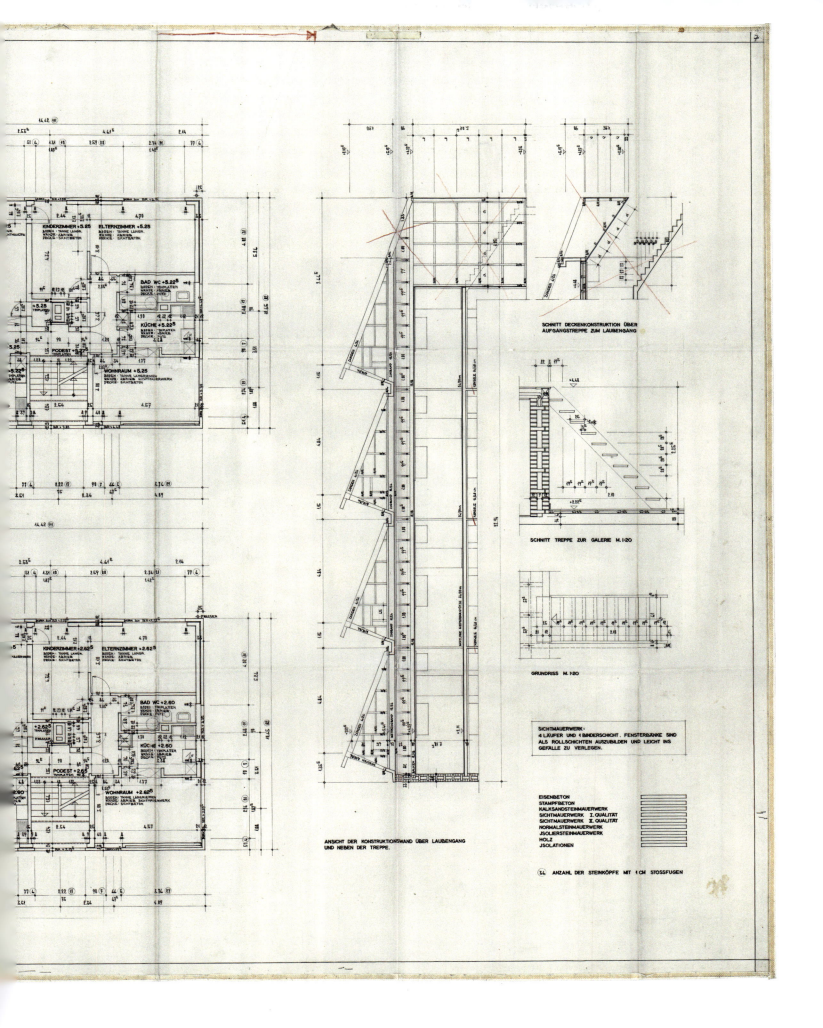

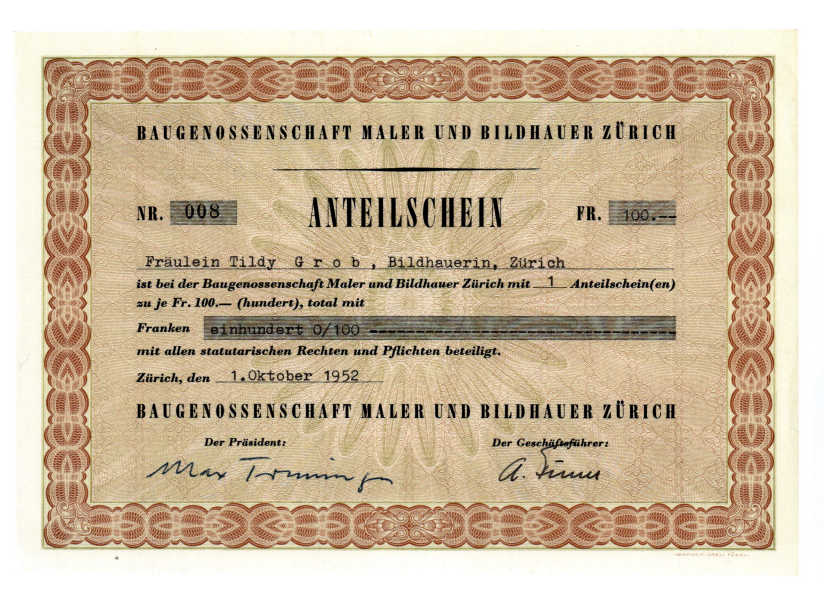

Share No. 008 of the Zurich Building Cooperative of
Painters and Sculptors, October 1, 1952

Stages of construction, home and studio wing, 1952/53

The almost finished building with rooftop tree to celebrate,
1952/53

Auszug
aus dem Protokolle des Stadtrates von Zürich
vom 16. Mai 1952.

1002. Grundpfanddarlehen an die Baugenossenschaft Maler und Bildhauer.

Ueber den Mangel an Arbeitsräumen für die bildenden Künstler ist schon wiederholt berichtet worden. Es kann auf die Antwort des Stadtrates auf die Schriftliche Anfrage von H. U. Fröhlich vom 21. Juni 1950 und auf die Vorlage über ein zinsfreies Darlehen für provisorische Ateliers an der Südstraße verwiesen werden.

Der Stadtrat vertrat damals die Meinung, daß die Schaffung weiterer Künstlerateliers auch in Zukunft gefördert werden müsse. Zu begrüßen ist, daß die Künstler in letzter Zeit verschiedentlich versucht haben, sich selber zu helfen und etwas zu unternehmen. Es sei an die Erstellung einiger Ateliers in einem dem Kanton gehörenden Oekonomiegebäude an der Südstraße erinnert, für welche der Gemeinderat am 27. Februar 1952 ein zinsfreies Darlehen gewährt hat.

Das gegenwärtig vorliegende Projekt eines Wohn- und Ateliergebäudes an der Wuhrstraße, Zürich 3, wird in weitgehendem Maße den Bedürfnissen nach weiteren Arbeitsräumen nicht nur vorübergehend, sondern auf lange Sicht entsprechen, indem in Verbindung mit 11 Ateliers 8 Wohnungen erstellt werden. Das Projekt stammt von Architekt Ernst Gisel, das in Zusammenarbeit mit dem städtischen Hochbauamt und den beteiligten Künstlern geschaffen wurde. In einem vierstöckigen Wohntrakt sind 4 Wohnungen zu 4 Zimmern und 4 Wohnungen zu 2 Zimmern, sowie im Dachstock noch 2 große und 2 kleinere Schülerateliers vorgesehen. Der zweigeschossige Ateliertrakt enthält im Erdgeschoß 4 Bildhauerateliers mit je einem Arbeitsraum von 50 m², einem Nebenraum von 12 m², Windfang und Abort. Im Obergeschoß sind 4 von einer Galerie aus zugängliche Malerateliers untergebracht, die einen Arbeitsraum von 34 m², einen Abort und auf einer Estrade weitere Räumlichkeiten von 8 m² und 7,7 m² aufweisen. Die Kosten belaufen sich für Gebäude und Umgebung auf Fr. 267 500 für den Wohntrakt und Fr. 195 500 für den Ateliertrakt, zusammen auf Fr. 463 000.

So erfreulich die eigenen Bemühungen der beteiligten Künstlerschaft sind, ist es leider unmöglich, das Bauvorhaben ohne namhafte finanzielle Mithilfe der Oeffentlichkeit durchzuführen. Enmal ist vorgesehen, das der Stadt gehörende Bauland an der Wuhrstraße, das 1286 m² mißt, der Genossenschaft Maler und Bildhauer im Baurecht auf die Dauer von

80 Jahren gegen einen Baurechtszins von 3½ % zur Verfügung zu stellen. Hierüber wurde am 24. März 1952 ein Vertrag öffentlich beurkundet. Aus den Krediten des Kantons und der Stadt für Wohnbauförderung waren an die 8 Wohnungen Beiträge in der Höhe von Fr. 48 000 erhältlich. An die Finanzierung der Nettoanlagekosten von Fr. 415 000 bringt die Genossenschaft Fr. 28 000 auf. Es ist vorgesehen, daß die Stadt ein Grundpfanddarlehen von Fr. 277 000 im ersten Rang gewährt, das verzinst und derart amortisiert werden soll, daß es nach Ablauf des Baurechtsvertrages getilgt ist. Für ein Grundpfanddarlehen von Fr. 110 000 im zweiten Rang wird zur Erzielung tragbarer Mietzinse um Zinsbefreiung nachgesucht. Auch dieses Darlehen würde innert 80 Jahren getilgt. Die Zinsentlastung für die zweite Hypothek, die Subventionen und der Zinszuschuß für die Wohnungen würden gestatten, die Wohnungen und Ateliers zu tragbaren Mietzinsen an die Mitglieder der Genossenschaft abzugeben, nämlich

		Fr.
4 Wohnungen zu 4 Zimmern	zu je	1 600
4 Wohnungen zu 2 Zimmern	» »	1 200
4 Bildhauer-Ateliers	» »	1 000
4 Maler-Ateliers	» »	900
4 Maler-Ateliers	» »	700
2 kleine Ateliers	» »	500

Mit einer verhältnismäßig bescheidenen Hilfe, die durch die Amortisation von Jahr zu Jahr geringer wird, kann mit diesem Projekt dem Mangel an Arbeitsräumen für Künstler in fühlbarer Weise und auf lange Sicht begegnet werden.

Auf den Antrag des Finanzvorstandes beschließt der Stadtrat:

1. Dem Gemeinderat wird beantragt:

Der Baugenossenschaft Maler und Bildhauer wird für die Erstellung eines Wohn- und Ateliergebäudes an der Wuhrstraße, Zürich 3, ein zinsfreies, innerhalb 80 Jahren zu tilgendes Grundpfanddarlehen im zweiten Rang von Fr. 110 000 gewährt.

2. Die Berichterstattung im Gemeinderat ist dem Finanzvorstand übertragen.

3. Der Finanzvorstand wird eingeladen, nach Eintritt der Rechtskraft des Beschlusses des Gemeinderates dem Stadtrat den Darlehensvertrag zur Genehmigung vorzulegen.

4. Mitteilung an die Vorstände des Finanz- und des Bauamtes II, die Liegenschaftenverwaltung, das Büro für Wohnungsbau (2), das Hochbauamt und durch Weisung an den Gemeinderat.

Für getreuen Auszug
der Stadtschreiber

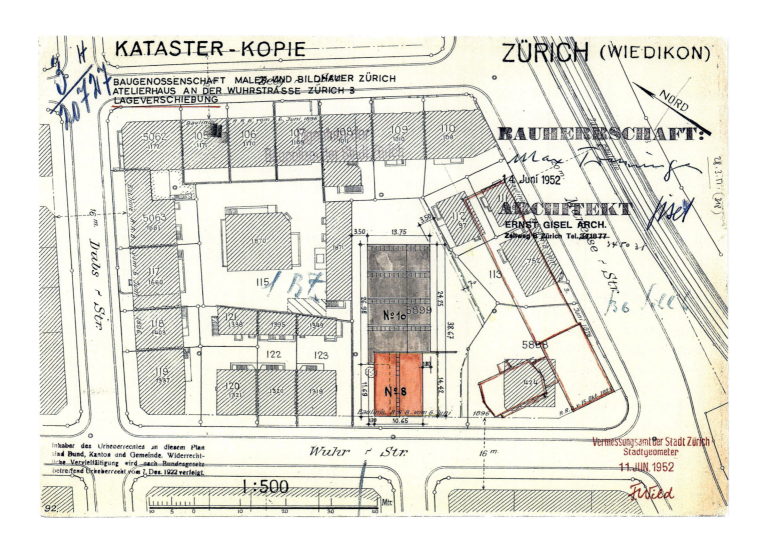

Land registry document showing the location of
Wuhrstrasse 8 and 10 (as well as the neighboring
building, still in the planning stage), June 14, 1952

Inauguration of the Zurich Building Cooperative of Painters and Sculptors, spring 1953

1   Ernst Gisel in conversation with painter and graphic artist Max Truninger, one of four initiators of the cooperative and its first president
2   Art historian Marianne Gisel with city mayor Emil Landolt
3   Ernst Gisel in conversation with Max Truninger and attorney Robert Meyer
4   Unidentified guests
5   Max Truninger (2nd from left), city councilor Heinrich Oetiker, attorney Robert Meyer, Ernst Gisel, and city councilor Jakob Peter (the latter two with their backs to the camera)
6   Painter, sculptor, and graphic artist Carlo Vivarelli with Max Truninger (2nd and 3rd from left) and guests

1 Carlo Vivarelli and his wife Elvira
2 Elvira Vivarelli and art dealer Henri Wengér
3 Sculptors and painters Regina de Vries and Tildy Grob-Wengér
4 Architect Alfred Roth (left), viewing one of the apartments
5 Ernst and Marianne Gisel
6 A beaming Ernst Gisel

1   Sculptor Hermana Morach-Sjövall with her husband, painter Otto Morach
2   Otto Müller, one of the four initiators of the cooperative, with sculptor and painter Trudi Demut and guests
3   Marianne Gisel in conversation with an unidentified guest

4   Sculptor Otto Teucher (in the center, smoking), one of the four initiators of the cooperative in conversation with Regina de Vries
5   Architect Robert Winkler and his wife Renée in conversation with Marianne and Ernst Gisel
6   Ernst Gisel during the introductory speech at the inauguration of the cooperative

One of the attic studios in the building, furnished for the inauguration

Aus dem Atelierhaus an der Wuhrstraße, Zürich. Bildhaueratelier | Maison des artistes à Zurich; atelier de sculpteur | Group of artist-studios in Zürich, studio of a sculptor

Künstlerateliers

Ateliers d'artiste | Artist-studios

Mit dem Problem der Künstlerateliers befaßte sich das WERK in zusammenhängender Form erstmals im Dezemberheft 1948. «Wer soll Künstlerateliers bauen?» hieß die damalige Fragestellung. Unsere Mahnungen fanden erfreulicherweise Gehör, und wir veröffentlichen in dem vorliegenden Heft ein erstes Ergebnis des Vorstoßes in Form des Künstlerhauses in Zürich. Ferner enthält das Heft einzelne Künstlerhäuser und in der Chronik ein leider nicht zur Ausführung gekommenes Projekt einer Künstlersiedlung der Architekten Frisch und Trösch in Zürich. Red.

Atelierhaus an der Wuhrstraße in Zürich

1953/54, Ernst Gisel, Architekt BSA/SIA, Zürich

Verschiedene Maler und Bildhauer sowie zahlreiche Gönner dieser Künstler haben sich zu einer Genossenschaft zusammengeschlossen, die den Bau von Ateliers zum Ziel hat.

Es ist der Genossenschaft in enger Fühlungnahme mit dem Hochbauamt der Stadt Zürich und mit dem Finanzamt gelungen, das vorliegende Gebäude zu realisieren. Das an der Wuhrstraße von der Stadt Zürich im Baurecht zur Verfügung gestellte Land erlaubte den Bau von 8 Wohnungen und 12 Ateliers.

Grundlegend für die Projektierung war die Rücksicht auf eine möglichst gute Belichtung der Arbeitsräume, denn das Grundstück ist auf drei Seiten von hohen Bauten eingeschlossen. Die Ausführung mußte äußerst ökonomisch sein. Die Anlage gliedert sich in das an der Straße gelegene Wohnhaus und den dahinterliegenden Ateliertrakt. Das Wohnhaus enthält auf 4 Geschossen je 2 Wohnungen und im 5. Geschoß 2 große Ateliers mit Oberlicht und 2 kleinere mit Seitenlicht.

Im hinteren Teil sind ebenerdig 4 Bildhauerateliers aneinandergereiht. Darüber liegen, von einem Laubengang aus erschlossen, 4 Malerateliers. Für den Ateliertrakt wurde ein möglichst knapper Grundriß gesucht, um den Bildhauern einen großen Werkplatz im Freien zu sichern. Dieser ist von einer 2,40 m hohen Betonmauer umschlossen.

Das Wohnhaus ist aus Backsteinen sichtbar gemauert und wird durch die Fensterflächen mit den außen aufgesetzten Rolladenkasten belebt. Auch im Ateliertrakt bestehen die Mauern aus unverputztem Backstein. Der Laubengang ist aus sichtbarem Eisenbeton konstruiert, und die Oberlichtdreiecke sind mit Eternit verschalt. Alle Dächer sind mit großwelligem Eternit eingedeckt.

Bei den Atelierräumen sind die Mauern auch im Innern unverputzt geblieben und geweißelt. Die Decken sind in einfacher Holzkonstruktion als Shed ausgebildet und mit Gipsplatten verkleidet. Holzwände sind in Grautönen lasierend gestrichen. Die Ateliers werden durch das schräggestellte

6

Dachdetail | Toiture; détail | Roof detail
Photo: Walter Binder, Zürich

Photos: Hans Finsler SWB, Zürich

Gesamtansicht der Ateliers und des Wohnbaus von Osten | Les ateliers d'artistes et l'immeuble d'appartements; vue prise de l'est | The artist-studios and the apartment block, from the east

Der Wohnbau, Fassade Wuhrstraße | Le bâtiment d'habitation; façade sud-ouest | South-west elevation of the apartment block

Die Ateliers von oben, l. Bildhauer, r. oben Maler | Les ateliers, à g. pour sculpteurs, à dr. et en h. pour peintres; vue prise du nord | The artist-studios from the north, at l. for sculptors, at r. and on first floor level for painters

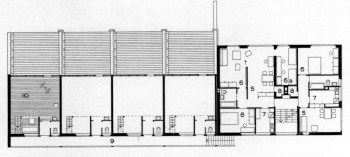

Erstes Obergeschoß mit Laubengang zu den Malerateliers 1:400 / Etage; à g., les ateliers de peintres, à dr., appartements / Upper floor, at l., studios for artist-painters, at r., apartments

Dachgeschoß Wohnbau mit Ateliers 1:400 / 4e étage du bâtiment d'habitation / Foorth floor of apartment block

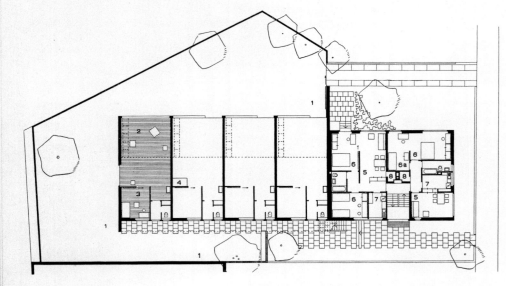

Erdgeschoß 1:400, l. Bildhauerateliers / Rez-de-chaussée; à g., ateliers pour sculpteurs / Ground-floor, at l., studios for sculptors

1 Werkplätze Bildhauer
2 Bildhaueratelier
3 Nebenraum
4 Lehmgrube
5 Eß- und Wohnraum
6 Schlaf- und Arbeitsraum
6a Kann je nach Bedarf zur linken oder rechten Wohnung gehören
7 Küche
8 Schrankraum
9 Laubengang
10 Maleratelier
11 Galerie Maleratelier
12 Abstellraum
13 Schülerateliers
14 Dusche

Lageplan 1:2000 / Plan de situation / Site plan

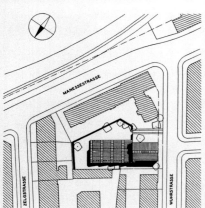

Aus einer Wohnung / Détail d'un appartement / Part of an apartment

Links / A gauche / Left
Schnitt Wohnbau und Ateliers 1:400 / Coupe / Cross-section

Rechts / A droite / Right
Längsschnitt Ateliers / Coupe ateliers / Cross-section of studios

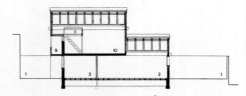

Atelier des Bildhauers Silvio Mattioli / Atelier du sculpteur Silvio Mattioli / Studio of the sculptor Silvio Mattioli   Photos: Hans Finsler SWB, Zürich

Oberlicht erhellt. Die Bildhauerateliers weisen ein zusätzliches Seitenlicht auf. In den Malerateliers wird der direkte Ausblick durch kleine Fenster ermöglicht, welche die Hauptlichtquelle nicht konkurrenzieren. In den Malerateliers ist eine Galerie eingebaut worden, die den Laubengang überdeckt. Den Bildhauerateliers sind geräumige Nebenräume angegliedert. Jedes Atelier hat seinen Vorraum und die nötigen sanitären Einrichtungen. Für die Wohnungen wurde ein sehr beweglicher Grundriß entwickelt. In jeder Etage, die zwei verschiedene Wohnungstypen enthält, ist eines der Zimmer so angeordnet, daß es je nach Bedarf zur einen oder anderen Wohnung geschlagen werden kann. So entstehen entweder zwei Dreizimmerwohnungen oder eine Zwei- und Vierzimmerwohnung. Bei aller Einfachheit sind die Wohnungen räumlich möglichst großzügig durchgebildet. Im einen Wohnungstyp können zwei Zimmer durch eine Schiebwand zu einem einzigen großen Raum verbunden werden. Die Fenster sind reichlich dimensioniert und gehen ohne Sturz bis unter die Decke. Die Mauern sind in den Wohnungen verputzt und abgerieben und mit abwaschbarer Emulsionsfarbe gestrichen. Wenige, räumlich bedeutungsvolle Wände sind aus Backstein sichtbar gemauert. Die Eisenbetondecken sind unverputzt und weiß gestrichen.

Trotz dem freien Grundriß der Wohnungen und dem Einbau von Schiebtüren, Schränken usw. beträgt der Kubikmeterpreis für das Wohnhaus Fr. 104.– inkl. Honorar, für den Ateliertrakt Fr. 75.– inkl. Honorar.   E.G.

Bildhaueratelier / Atelier de sculpteur / Studio of a sculptor

Ernst Gisel, *Atelierhaus Wuhrstrasse, Plan No. 1094*,
drawings of the southwest and northeast façades,
September 24, 1952

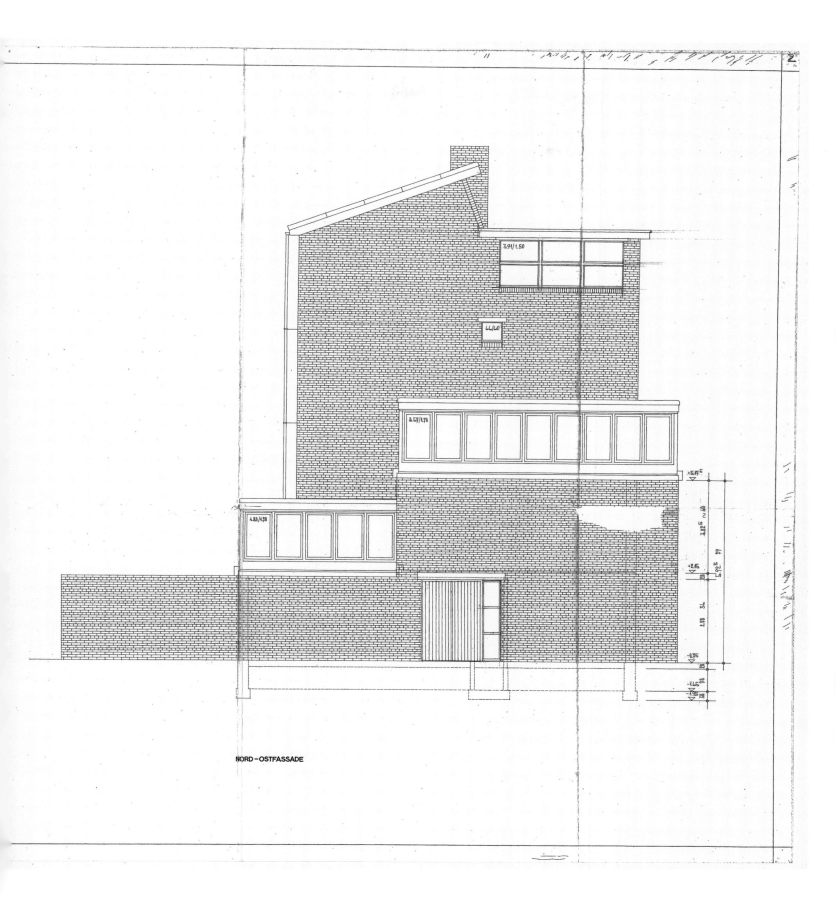

NORD-OSTFASSADE

Ernst Gisel, *Atelierhaus Wuhrstrasse, Plan No. 1093*, drawings of the southeast façades, September 4, 1952

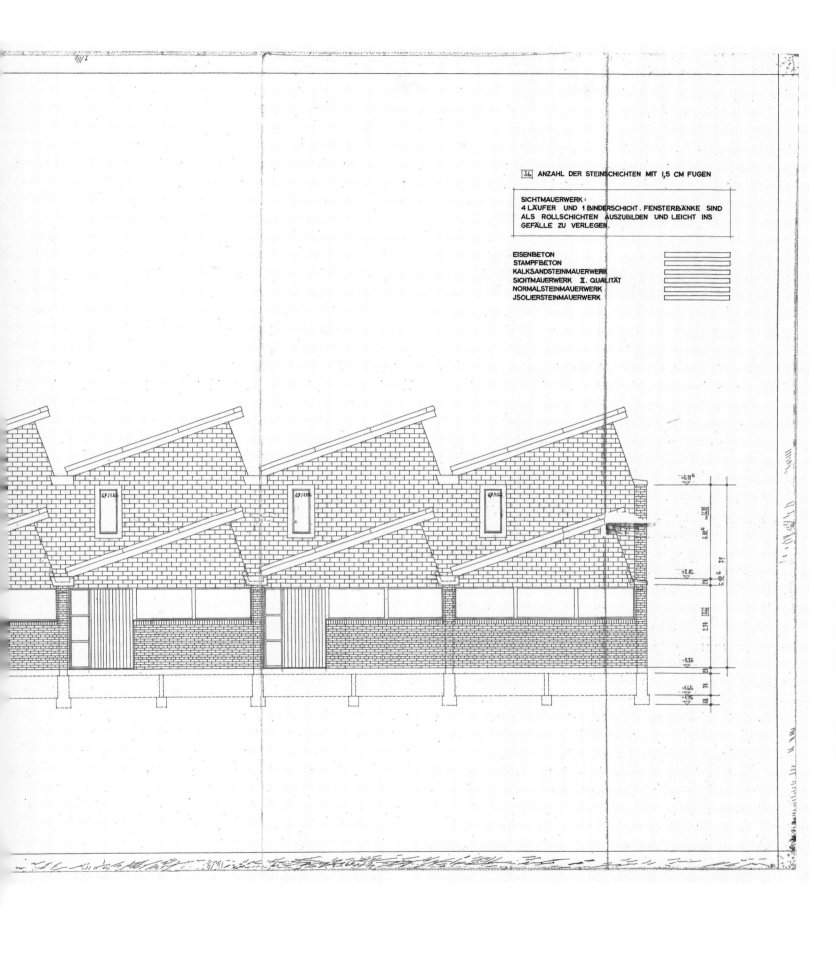

Ernst Gisel, *Atelierhaus Wuhrstrasse, Plan No. 1095*,
drawings of the northwest façades, September 16, 1952

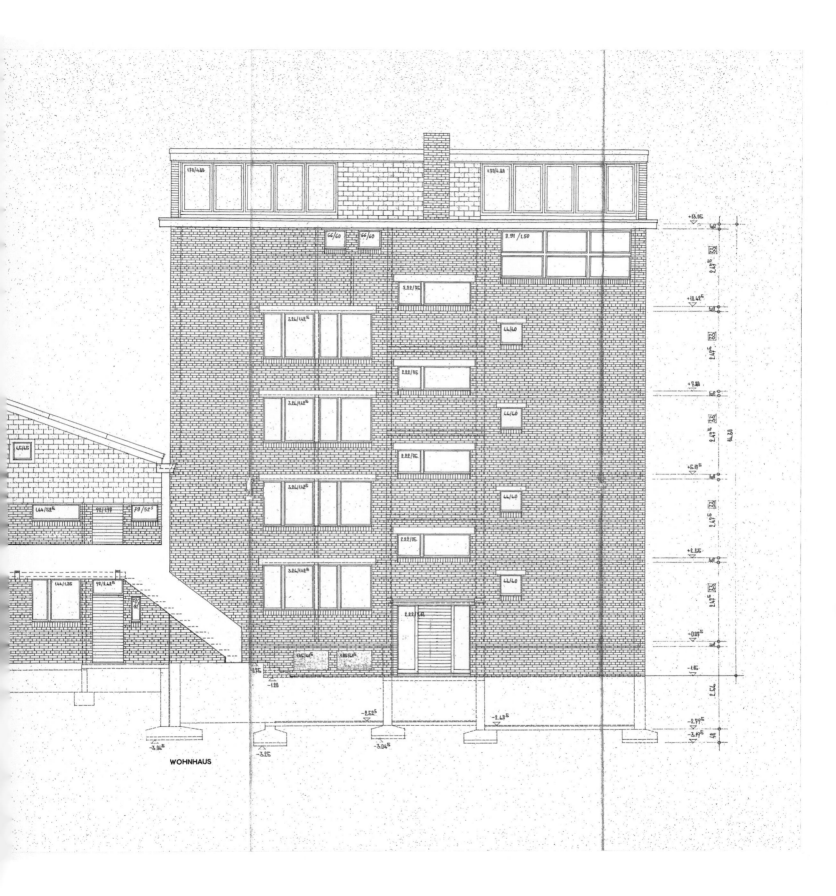

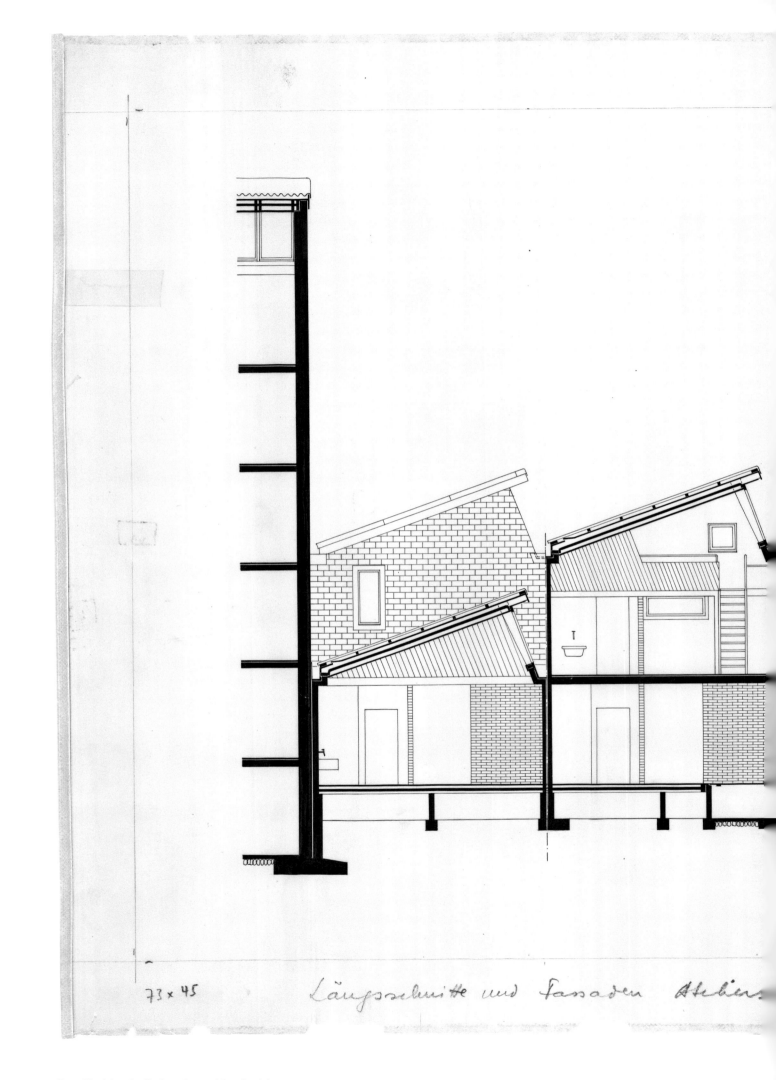

Ernst Gisel, longitudinal section and façade of the courtyard studios, architectural drawing, 1952

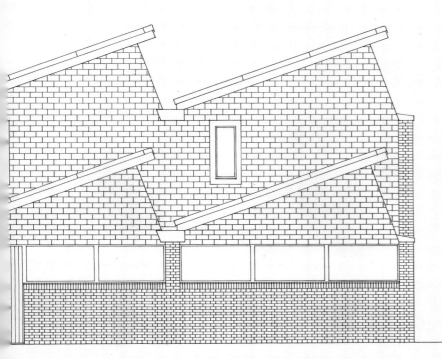

140-052.3

Cooperative shortly after completion, spring 1953

Interior view of one of the apartments from a series of photographs by the pioneer of new photography, Hans Finsler, upon completion of the cooperative, 1953

Otto Teucher's studio, from a series of photographs made by Hans Finsler upon completion of the cooperative, 1953

Ernst Gisel with students in Otto Teucher's studio, 1953

Mit der Zunahme der Wohnungsnot verschärfte sich für die Zürcher Maler und Bildhauer auch unaufhaltsam das Problem, ein geeignetes Atelier zu finden. Mit echt künstlerischem Temperament sind sie nun dieser Sorge zu Leibe gerückt. Schon 1949 hatten sich einige von ihnen zu einer Genossenschaft zusammengeschlossen, ihre Sparbatzen auf ein Häufchen gelegt und den Stadtvätern einen beherzten Brief geschrieben, etwa des Inhalts, dass sie nun genug von der ewigen Kalamität mit schlechtbeleuchteten Dachkammern und keifenden Zimmervermieterinnen hätten und selbst bauen möchten, vorausgesetzt ... Sie hatten richtig vorausgesetzt: die Stadtväter hatten Musikgehör und machten mit! Sie haben Sinn für das Zürcher Kunstleben und hofften wohl, unter einem festgefügten Dach auch einen soliden Kern seiner Vertreter unterzubringen und damit festzuhalten. Die Stadt griff tief in ihr Portemonnaie und half — zusammen mit dem

Fräulein Trudi Demut empfängt uns mit der Befangenheit der jungen Künstlerin, die das Vorurteil der eindringenden «Banausen» befürchtet. Nach einer kaufmännischen Lehre, die sie auf Wunsch ihrer Eltern absolvierte, besuchte sie in England eine Modellierklasse und widmet sich nun mit voller Hingabe der Bildhauerei.

Aufnahmen: Dr. E. Bleuler

Harmonie ist ein Begriff sowohl aus dem Reich der Töne, als auch aus dem der Farben. Der lebende Beweis für das Verbindende zwischen den beiden Künsten sind die Eheleute Frau Lotte Krafft, Geigerin im Tonhalle-Orchester, und der Maler Hans Rohner. Die Wohnung ist mit dem Atelier durch eine Treppe verbunden, die Herr Rohner alle mal in der stolzen Illusion des auf Deck steigenden Kapitäns erklettert.

Zürcher Künstler beziehen ein eigenes Heim

Links: Das Künstlerheim an der Wuhrstrasse mit den «gebrochenen» Giebeln, in denen die Ateliers eingebaut sind.

Auf unsere Frage, wie ihm die neue Wohnung gefalle, antwortete der Grafiker Carlo Vivarelli lachend: «Vorbehaltlos, wie eine junge Braut.» Auch seine charmante Frau ist glücklich im eben bezogenen Heim und hofft nur, dass die beiden prächtigen Tannen vor ihren Fenstern dem in der Nähe projektierten Neubau nicht zum Opfer fallen.

Kanton — in Form von Subventionen oder unverzinslichen Darlehen nach.

Wer heute im Wiedikoner Quartier die Wuhrstrasse passiert, bemerkt die in sauberem Backstein gehaltene, originelle Fassade des eben von den beteiligten Künstlern bezogenen Neubaus. Nach dem Entwurf von Architekt Ernst Gisler entstanden acht Wohnungen zu zwei bis vier Zimmern, raffiniert ineinander verschachtelt; dazu kommen acht helle Ateliers, unten für die Bildhauer, oben für die Maler, Räume, die auch zum Wohnen sich eignen. Stolz und glücklich über das gelungene Gemeinschaftswerk haben sich die Künstler zum grösseren Teil bereits wohnlich installiert und hoffen, dass sie unter den neugeschaffenen Voraussetzungen auch in künstlerischer Hinsicht mehr und Besseres zu leisten vermögen.

Der Bildhauer Otto Müller gehört mit Architekt Gisler zu den Hauptinitianten des wohlgelungenen Genossenschaftswerkes und er freut sich nun doppelt seines neuen Ateliers, in welchem er nun auch rein räumlich seine Arbeiten mit der nötigen Distanz betrachten kann.

Oskar Dalvit ist ein bekannter Maler der expressionistischen Richtung. Er äussert sich wie alle anderen begeistert über seinen neuen Arbeitsraum. «Ein Atelier darf den Schaffenden nicht beengen, er muss atmen und sich bewegen können.»

Schweizer Familien-Wochenblatt, August 1, 1953

Tildy Grob-Wengér, nicknamed *Pierrot*, early 1950s

Tildy Grob-Wengér in her apartment, c. 1960 **Henri Wengér and Tildy Grob-Wengér's apartment, 1958**

Painter Carlotta Stocker making collages in her studio
with Mia, the cooperative's cat, in the foreground, c. 1955

Trudi Demut with limestone sculpture, *Figur 1*,
Otto Müller's courtyard workshop, 1960

MEMBERS 1953–2021

Who	Life Data	When	Studio	Apartment
Hans Aeschbacher	1906–1980	1953–1965		1953–1965
Luigi Archetti	*1955	2013–	2013–	
Patricia Bucher	*1976	2020–		2020–
René Ed. Brauchli	1934–2005	1965–2005	1968–2005	1965–1982 / 2003–2005
Marlyse Brunner	*1946	1981–1982	1981–1982	
Stefan Burger	*1977	2010–	2012–	2010–
Oskar Dalvit	1911–1975	1953–1968	1953–1968	
Doris Dedual-Koller	*1949	1987–	1987–	1989–
Trudi Demut	1927–2000	1953–2000	1953–2000	
Urs Frei	*1958	2001–	2001–	
Katrin Freisager	*1960	2018–2019	2018–2019	
Andrea Gohl	*1970	2005–	2011–	2005–
Ruedi Gregor	1944–1984	1977–1984		1977–1984
Tildy Grob-Wengér	1914–2012	1953–2006	1955–2006	1953–2007
Franz Grossert y Cañameras	1936–2009	1972–1978	1972–1978	
Rudolf Günthardt	1925–1976	1973–1976	1973–1976	
Edi Hebeisen	1959–2012	1994–2012	1997–2012	1994–2007
Irma Hediger	*1936	1987–1993	1989–1993	1987–1993
Bruno Heller	1925–2014	1953–1959	1953–1959	1953–1959
Alfred Huber	1908–1982	1957–1965		1957–1965
Rainer Klausmann	*1949	1980–		1980–
Ödön Koch	1906–1977	1971–1977		1971–1977
Friedrich Kuhn	1926–1972	1959–1972	1959–1972	
Zilla Leutenegger	*1968	2015–	2015–	
William Lutz	*1949	1988–	1993–	1988–
Anja Maissen	1964–2013	2006–2013	2011–2013	2006–2013
Pietro Mattioli	*1957	1993–	1993–	1993–
Silvio Mattioli	1929–2011	1953–1972	1953–1972	1959–1970

Who	Life data	When	Studio	Apartment
Hansjörg Mattmüller	1923–2006	1973–2004	1973–2004	1982–2002
Doris Michel	*1948	1992–	1992–	
Hermana Morach-Sjövall	1899–1974	1953–1974	1953–1955	1953–1974
Otto Morach	1878–1973	1953–1973	1953–1973	1953–1973
Otto Müller	1905–1993	1953–1993	1953–1993	
Caroline Palla	*1969	2019–	2019–	
David Renggli	*1974	2007–2011	2007–2011	2007–2009
Hans Rohner	1898–1972	1953–1972	1953–1972	1953–1972
Remo Roth	*1934	1974–2012	1974–2012	
Klaudia Schifferle	*1955	1988/1989	1988/1989	1988/1989
Bert Schmidmeister	1934–1993	1968–1993	1972–1993	1968–1980
Heinrich Senn	1930–2004	1965–1968		1965–1968
Veronika Spierenburg	*1981	2015–		2015–
Valeria Stefané-Klausmann	*1948	1980–	1989–	1980–
Peter Stiefel	1942–2019	1982–1989	1984–1989	1982–1988
Carlotta Stocker	1921–1972	1953–1972	1953–1972	1970–1971
Otto Teucher	1899–1994	1953–1994	1953–1994	1953–1994
Andrea Thal	*1975	2007–2015		2007–2015
Peter Trachsel	1949–2013	1984–1987		1984–1987
Carlo Vivarelli	1919–1986	1953–1986	1953–1986	1953–1986
Henri Wengér	1914–1972	1953–1972	1971/1972	1953–1972
Mirjam Wirz	*1973	2014–2018	2014–2018	
Werner W. Wyss	1926–2014	1974–2014	1976–2014	1974–1988
Gertrud Zöllig	?	1972/1973	1972/1973	
Robert Zuberbühler	?	1953–1957		1953–1957

Presidents

Who	Life data	When		
Max Trunninger	1910–1986	1948–1966		
Otto Teucher		1966–1984		
Carlo Vivarelli		1984–1986		
René Ed. Brauchli		1986–2002		
Pietro Mattioli		2002–		

Auch Maler müssen ein Dach über

Sauerstoffflasche und Schweißapparat gehören zu den unentbehrlichen Utensilien des modernen Plastikers. Im Hinterhof ist der junge Silvio Mattioli damit beschäftigt, eine seiner pflanzenhaften Eisenplastiken zusammenzufügen, die aus Paul Klees Zaubergarten aufzublühen scheinen. Im Hintergrund wartet ein Schulhausbrunnen auf seine Vollendung. Mattioli lebt mit Frau und Kind in seinem Atelier.

Stoff für ein surrealistisches Stilleben: in einer verlassenen Ecke des Hofes geben sich ein halbvollendeter Männerkopf, ein Hammer, ein verstaubter Spiegel und die Anfänge (oder Überreste) einer abstrakten Plastik ein Stelldichein, wie es sich Giorgio de Chirico nicht magischer wünschen könnte.

Eine Voliere hat die Plastikerin und Malerin Tildy Grob sowohl aus ihrer reizvoll-originellen Wohnung, in der ein Dutzend Wellensittiche frei herumflattern, wie auch aus ihrem Atelier unter dem Dachstock gemacht. Privat ist Tildy Grob Mme Wenger – Gattin des Gérants der Librairie Française.

Zürcher Künstler griffen zur Selbsthilfe

Wenn wir schon klagen, daß es erstens zu wenig Wohnungen gibt und zweitens zu hohe Mieten verlangt werden, was sollen da erst die Maler und Bildhauer sagen? Sie benötigen nicht nur Raum, um zu leben, sondern auch, um arbeiten zu können. Zur Wohnungs- kommt die Ateliersorge. Von kunstfreundlich gesinnten Hausbesitzern hört man selten, um so häufiger hingegen von solchen, die Wert auf ein regelmäßiges Einkommen ihrer Mieter legen. Und auch auf einen seriösen Lebenswandel. Doch der Letzte im Monat, der in den bürgerlichen Berufen Zahltag heißt, ist für Künstler genau so ein Tag wie jeder andere. Außerdem gelten sie bekanntlich – obschon meist zu Unrecht – als ein lockeres Völkchen. Aber auch Maler benötigen ein Dach über dem Kopfe. Wundert man sich noch, daß sie da zur Selbsthilfe griffen?

Zürcher Maler und Plastiker schlossen sich zu einer Genossenschaft zusammen. Was sie wollten, stand von Anfang an fest: Wohnungen und Ateliers gemäß ihren Bedürfnissen. Woher jedoch das Geld nehmen? Hilfe war vonnöten, und sie konnte nur von *einer* Seite her kommen: von der öffentlichen Hand. Also gelangte man an sie, welche ihre Unterstützung schließlich in großzügiger Form gewährt hat, nachdem sie sich zuerst bitten ließ, wie es sich gehört. Sie stellte in einem Außenquartier den Boden zur Verfügung, half den Bau finanzieren – nicht ganz umsonst, soviel Generosität darf man von ihr auch nicht verlangen, doch unter der leicht zu erfüllenden Bedingung, daß die Gebäulichkeiten nach achtzig Jahren in ihren Besitz übergehen würden. Den Beitrag an das Genossenschaftskapital selber konnte man für jedes Mitglied auf die Höhe eines Jahreszinses beschränken.

Nach Plänen von Ernst Gisel wurde zu bauen begonnen. Dem gegen die Straße hin gelegenen Wohnhaus ließ der Architekt den Ateliertrakt folgen, zweigeschossig mit kleineren Malerwerkstätten auf der einen Seite, eingeschossig mit größeren Arbeitsräumen für Bildhauer auf der andern: eine ebenso einfache wie vernünftige Lösung. Vor etwa dreieinhalb Jahren konnte der Bau bezogen werden. Zürich erhielt seine erste Künstlerkolonie. Und inzwischen hat es sich herausgestellt, daß es sich darin leben läßt.

Die Ateliers haben alles, was nötig ist: viel Raum und viel Licht und die Möglichkeit, eine Atmosphäre zu schaffen. Für den Fall, daß die Arbeit ruht, besitzen sie eine stille Ecke mit Platz für ein Sofa, Tisch und Stuhl. Für jene Maler, die sich zu ihrer Werkstatt nicht auch noch eine selbständige Wohnung leisten können, ist Raum für eine kleine Küche vorhanden. Und wenn sie die schmale, hohe Treppe hinaufklettern, sind sie in ihrem Schlafzimmer. Ein paar an die Wand geheftete Reproduktionen, dazu die eigenen Bilder und Plastiken, einige schöne und seltene Dinge (Muschelsammlungen sind große Mode an der Wuhrstraße 10), vielleicht auch noch da und dort eine Topfpflanze, wie sie beim Maler Oscar Dalvit so pracht-

Der Ateliertrakt der Künstlerkolonie Wuhrstraße 10, dem sich links außen das Wohnhaus anschließt, beide gebaut von dem jungen Zürcher Architekten Ernst Gisel. Hohe Fenster sorgen für das nötige Licht in den Werkstätten, die günstige Arbeitsbedingungen, Geräumigkeit und Wohnlichkeit bieten und dazu nicht mehr als 70–90 Franken Miete im Monat kosten. Auch die 150 Franken für eine Dreizimmerwohnung sind für heutige Verhältnisse ein bescheidener Preis.

▶ **Die junge Malerin Carlotta Stocker,** Trägerin des C.-F.-Meyer-Preises, überraschten wir bei der Arbeit an einem Früchte- und Flaschenstilleben, das sie auf einer alten Kiste neben der Leinwand aufgebaut hatte. Sie malt nicht nur, sondern wohnt auch in ihrem Atelier. Was sie ihm vorwirft, ist einzig die poesielose Umgebung nüchterner Mietskasernen.

Aufnahmen Fred Mayer

◀ **Wenn Pinsel, Stift und Meißel ruhen,** bietet eine Wohnecke Gelegenheit zu Muße und Erholung oder auch, sich mit einem Besuch zu einer Tasse Kaffee zurückzuziehen: die Bildhauerin Tildy Demut (rechts außen) mit der Gattin und dem Söhnchen ihres Kollegen Hans Aschbacher. Die schmale Treppe führt zur Schlafnische hinauf, und neben der Türe findet noch eine kleine Küche Platz.

voll grünen – und schon darf man sich zuhause fühlen.

Kein Wunder, daß sich so viele Maler um ein Atelier oder eine Wohnung an der Wuhrstraße bewerben. Aber es will nichts frei werden: den bisherigen Mietern gefällt es viel zu gut und sie vertragen sich untereinander allen Voraussagen zum Trotz viel zu harmonisch, um auszuziehen. Warum also nicht eine zweite Künstlerkolonie bauen? Freilich – sie müßte wiederum innerhalb der Stadt gelegen sein, weil mancher Maler hier seine Schüler, eine Lehrstelle oder sonst eine Erwerbsquelle besitzt, die er verlieren würde, müßte er die Stadt verlassen. An Bestrebungen, eine weitere Malersiedlung zu gründen, fehlt es denn auch nicht. Hoffentlich dauert es nicht zu lange, bis sie Wirklichkeit werden – und die Öffentlichkeit einen Grund mehr besitzt, auf ihre Großzügigkeit stolz zu sein. Denn vermag sie den künstlerisch Schaffenden besser zu helfen, als indem sie ihnen günstige Lebens- und Arbeitsbedingungen ermöglicht?

F. L.

dem Kopf haben...

Wooden column by Silvio Mattioli in the finished courtyard workshop, autumn 1953

A SMALL UTOPIA
MATERIALIZES

CAROLINE KESSER

Wuhrstrasse is a telling address for this artists' cooperative. The street name comes from the German word *Wehr*, referring to the weir that once dammed up the river Sihl and in which another word resonates, the verb *wehren*, meaning to fight back or defend oneself.

It is unlikely that the founders of the Baugenossenschaft Maler und Bildhauer Zürich (the Painters and Sculptors Building Cooperative Zurich) would have succeeded without their fighting spirit, self-confidence, and persistence. Just imagine: three penniless artists pursue the ambitious goal of establishing a location for like-minded souls in the city of Zurich with reasonably priced flats and studios where they can work undisturbed and unrestricted. The three—sculptors Otto Müller and Otto Teucher, and painter Max Truninger—took matters into their own hands and decided to do something about the precarious postwar conditions that young artists in Zurich had to face. Sales and commissions were hard to come by and the rare affordable studio was largely in the form of temporary quarters in buildings awaiting demolition.

When the three registered their building cooperative of painters and sculptors, the Baugenossenschaft Maler und Bildhauer Zürich, in 1949, they already had the support of committed, influential patrons, most especially their friendship with the architect Ernst Gisel. A longtime champion of both cooperative efforts and art, he had planted the idea in the heads of the substantially older artists. Born in 1922, Gisel, who adopted their cause, had already proposed an (ideal) project for a painters' and sculptors' colony in 1948. He was also well-connected with representatives of the authorities, not least with Emil Landolt, Zurich's city president since 1949, and the cooperative was assured the support of the city's architect and urban planner Albert Heinrich Steiner as well as cantonal architect Heinrich Peter. The relevant authorities in both city and canton actually took pleasure in promoting cooperative working and living spaces for artists, a group with a dubious reputation among conventional building cooperatives. The image of the nonconformist, immoral artist was still so widespread that no self-respecting Swiss citizen would have welcomed being neighbor to a painter or sculptor. As a result, integrating artists' studios into a building development was usually nipped in the bud.

Müller, Teucher, and Truninger had the support of another notable patron, architect and journalist Alfred Roth, for whom Gisel had worked when he was twenty years old. In his article *"Wer soll Künstlerateliers bauen?"* (Who should build artists' studios?), published December 1948 in *Werk*, Roth put in a passionate plea for the building of publicly funded studios. For the co-author of the Werkbund Estate Neubühl (1932), which already had a few painters' studios, the artist was more than an individual to be integrated into society and the studio was not an ordinary architectural task: "It is a sacred place, where the noblest and most sublime endeavors a creative person can produce come to fruition."[1]

Having initially considered property on Dufourstrasse in the Seefeld district of Zurich, the city council subsequently offered the building cooperative a piece of land on Wuhrstrasse in Zurich-Wiedikon. In spring 1952, the parties signed a contract for an eighty-year lease on the property, comprising 13,840 square feet, with interest on building rights of 3–5 percent. The agreement included a building designed by Gisel containing eight apartments, as well as four studios for sculptors and four for painters. Construction commenced in July 1952 and the studios were ready for occupation in March 1953. The entire cost of construction amounted to 463,000 francs. The cooperative itself had only managed to raise 28,000 francs through contributions of 100 francs from each member of the cooperative plus the purchase of shares equaling one year's interest; the remainder was paid in full by city and canton. The tenants themselves managed the estate at Wuhrstrasse 8/10; a three-room apartment cost 150 francs and a studio 70 or 80. A representative of the city, who sat on the board, had a supervisory function.

Otto Müller and Otto Teucher immediately decided to share a sculptor's studio, but Max Truninger rented neither a studio nor a flat. His commitment to the cooperative had been purely idealistic and the success of this extraordinary project had benefited from the reputation he enjoyed with the city architect and other municipal authorities. He accepted the office of president of the cooperative for the same reason, which he held until 1966.

Trudi Demut, Tildy Grob and Henri Wengér, Silvio and Heidi Mattioli, Carlo and Elvira Vivarelli, Oskar Dalvit, Otto Morach, Hans Rohner and his wife, violinist Lotte Krafft were among the original residents. Hans Aeschbacher moved

---

[1] Alfred Roth, "Wer soll Künstlerateliers bauen?" in: *Werk* 35 (1948), vol. 12, pp. 369–374, p. 374.

Links: Die von Ernst Gisel erbaute Künstlerkolonie besteht aus einem Wohnhaus (im Hintergrund) und einem Ateliertrakt. Dem Doppelgeschoss mit den Malerwerkstätten sind die Bildhauerateliers vorgelagert.

Rechts: Die Plastikerin Tildy Demut hat sich mit ihrem Besuch — der Gattin ihres Kollegen Hans Aeschbacher — in die gemütliche Wohnecke zurückgezogen. Doch auch noch für eine Koch- und eine Schlafnische bieten die geräumigen Ateliers Platz.

WUHRSTRASSE 10
ZÜRICHS KÜNSTLERKOLONIE

Es genügt nicht, dass ein Maler seine Bilder, ein Plastiker seine Skulpturen ausstellen und gelegentlich verkaufen kann und ab und zu einen öffentlichen Auftrag erhält. Künstler müssen auch irgendwo arbeiten — ausser der Wohnung für sich und ihre Familie brauchen sie ein Atelier. Beides lässt sich heute schwer finden — und beides kostet Geld, oft mehr Geld, als ein Maler bei seinen unregelmässigen Einnahmen aufzubringen imstande ist.

Hinzu kommt, dass sich lange nicht jeder Raum als Werkstatt eignet. Ein Atelier braucht Licht, sehr viel Licht, das den Farben strahlendes Leben und den Formen Klarheit und Bestimmtheit schenkt. Gross und geräumig muss es ebenfalls sein. Die Staffelei, das Malwerkzeug, die angefangenen und die fertiggestellten Bilder, die Skizzen und Entwürfe, die Rahmen — das alles sollte untergebracht werden können. Und jeder Maler will seine Arbeiten nicht nur aus der Nähe,

◄ Im Atelier von Otto Müller begrüssen uns grosse, strenggeformte Frauenfiguren. Jede Ecke benötigt der Plastiker für seine Arbeiten, nicht einmal für eine Garderobe bleibt Raum — so müssen die halbvollendeten Statuen als Kleiderständer herhalten!

(Aufnahmen Fred Mayer)

Der junge Plastiker Silvio Mattioli ist meistens im Hintergrund anzutreffen, wo er seine abstrakten Skulpturen schmiedet: beim modernen Bildhauer ersetzt Eisen den Marmor, der Schweissapparat Meissel und Hammer.
▼

sondern auch aus Distanz betrachten und auf ihre Wirkung hin beurteilen. Dazu wünscht er sich eine Ecke, in der er sich erholen und sammeln kann. Als Stimmungsmensch ist er nicht unempfindlich gegenüber der Atmosphäre seiner Umgebung: sie vermag ihn in seinem Schaffen anzuspornen, aber auch zu lähmen — daher ist es nicht gleichgültig, in welcher Umwelt er arbeitet...

Um bei der herrschenden Raumknappheit nicht länger mit irgendeiner kleinen, engen und dunklen Dachmansarde vorlieb nehmen zu müssen, griffen vor einigen Jahren Zürcher Künstler zur Selbsthilfe, gründeten eine Genossenschaft, bauten eine Wohn- und Atelierkolonie, ohne Luxus, möglichst einfach, zweckmässig und billig. Dafür kostet eine Dreizimmerwohnung auch nur 150 Franken im Monat, ein Atelier nicht viel mehr als die Hälfte, und ist dabei so sinnvoll eingerichtet, dass es im Bedarfsfall auch als Wohn- und Schlafraum dienen kann. In jedem fühlt man sich zu Hause: noch kein einziges wechselte bisher seinen Mieter — dagegen melden sich immer mehr Interessenten. Vielleicht wird Zürich bald eine zweite Künstlerkolonie erhalten; wer die erste an der Wuhrstrasse 10 besucht hat, wird das Projekt freudig begrüssen.   ER

Als Modell für eines ihrer festlichen Stilleben hat Carlotta Stocker im Vordergrund einige Flaschen und eine Fruchtschale aufgestellt. Die begabte und bekannte Malerin zählt zu den prominenten Bewohnern der Zürcher Künstlerkolonie.

Die Bildhauerin und Malerin Tildy Grob hat ihren strengsten Kritiker in Jeannot, einem kleinen Kanarienvogel, gefunden. In ihrer originell eingerichteten Wohnung lässt die passionierte Vogelfreundin zudem ein Dutzend Wellensittiche frei herumflattern!

1+2 Sculptor Hans Aeschbacher in his apartment, Wuhrstrasse 8, c. 1957

3 Silvio Mattioli with *Herrscher Dunkler Gewässer,* Wuhrstrasse courtyard workshop, 1957

4 Friedrich Kuhn in his studio, 1960

Carlo Vivarelli working on *Zentrifugal*. Sculpture for the schoolhouse built by Jacques Schader, Eugen-Huber-Strasse, Zurich, 1964

into the last remaining flat with his wife Maja but continued to work at Wehntalerstrasse in the workshop he had shared with Otto Müller. Carlotta Stocker and Friedrich Kuhn joined soon afterwards, spicing up the atmosphere with such verve that the settlement soon became one of the most vibrant cultural hotspots in Zurich.

The Wuhrstrasse artists were not an exclusive coterie; they did not form a school nor did they represent a style. But there did emerge "a vibrant, mutually inspiring community," as envisioned by Alfred Roth, although not the "modern academy" that the Bauhaus admirer had hoped for. From the outset, it was a heterogeneous group in orientation, impact, and maturity. Morach was sixty-six when he moved in and preoccupied with his late work; Silvio Mattioli was twenty-four and fiercely striving to become one of Switzerland's leading iron sculptors. While Hans Aeschbacher could already be considered a "master," Otto Müller was moving ahead step by step in the process of finding his own inimitable idiom; he was awarded the art prize of the city of Zurich in 1985. And while Trudi Demut, once Müller's student, was gradually probing independence, Carlotta Stocker and Friedrich Kuhn were at the height of their creative powers. Carlo Vivarelli was already a well-known graphic artist on the cusp of becoming a concrete painter. Otto Teucher, who had moved in with two daughters, quietly and steadily continued to pursue his sculptural practice while teaching at the School of Applied Arts.

The battle that had been raging for decades between abstract/concrete and figurative art did not affect the Wuhrstrasse. The two camps were peacefully united there: *Schule der "kleinen Wahnwelt"* (School of "Mini Madness"), as Paul Nizon dubbed the movement around Friedrich Kuhn, met with the same appreciation as the constructive art embodied by Vivarelli, which had— at least temporarily—influenced other protagonists in the colony, among them Otto Müller, Hans Aeschbacher, Otto Teucher, Trudi Demut, and short-term resident Odön Koch.

At times, things did get out of hand at Wuhrstrasse 8/10, what with the wild hammering and welding, the temper tantrums of certain residents, and the rowdy partying. In the early days, disgruntled neighbors kept calling the police. Even so, the members of the cooperative consistently showed an enlightened attitude of mutual respect. This had an impact on the neighborhood as well, where they soon won the appreciation and respect of their neighbors. Despite inevitable rivalry, power struggles, and intrigue, the cooperative spirit always prevailed. Periodical outbreaks did not prevent initiators from regularly taking stock of what it takes to live together in a cooperative, a model to which their building and their small, lived utopia was indebted. As long-term vice president, Otto Müller kept reminding the members to show mutual consideration. Tolerance was and is a prerequisite at Wuhrstrasse, where people live close together, the walls are thin, and one cannot help hearing what's happening next door. It is not surprising that Aeschbacher's rampages were hard to take. In 1965 he and his family moved into a house of their own in Russikon. They had three small daughters by then, and it was clearly time for Maja to leave the cooperative.

Tildy Grob-Wengér has been living at Wuhrstrasse for fifty years and looking back, surprised herself on realizing that, as far as she knew, there had never been difficulties. The sculptor and painter, known as "Miss Wuhri" for her unusual beauty, emphasizes that people always respected each other. She was married to Henri Wengér, director of the Librairie française and later owner of the Henri Wengér bookstore and gallery. Her social life in the cooperative was characterized by a certain detachment since she worked with her husband in the bookstore; they were oriented primarily toward Paris and cultivated a circle of friends that included renowned artists, writers, and actors. They would occasionally have visitors from Paris at Wuhrstrasse. Ionesco made drawings in their studio with great enthusiasm but with no artistic pretensions so that his hostess did not save them, for they seemed to her to be somewhat clumsy creations.

Contact among individuals and groups was not based on a binding ideology. People who wanted to work quietly and on their own were left in peace. Everyone respected Otto Morach and did not take umbrage at the fact that they hardly ever saw this friendly man, who had belonged to the avant-garde at the time of the First World War. However, they had no trouble hearing him since it seems that he always kicked the door closed instead of using the handle. The other residents sorely missed these acoustic signals when he died.

Otto Müller working on the relief *Grosse Messingtafel*, Wuhrstrasse courtyard workshop, 1972

Carlotta Stocker in her studio in front of a collage mock-up of the ceramic mural for the Children's Hospital in Zurich, 1968

The sense of community always rose to the challenge when someone was not well, as Maya Vautier Schmidmeister recalls. She moved in with Bert Schmidmeister in 1968 and gave birth to her son Simon at Wuhrstrasse. Despite his unbridled temperament and hopeless alcoholism, everyone accepted the painter Schmidmeister. When he deteriorated even more and could no longer pay the rent, the cooperative carried the cost.

In retrospect, Maya Vautier sees herself as a kind of "concierge" at Wuhrstrasse—a role that she rather enjoyed playing until she moved out in 1979. She lived in a ground-floor flat with a small child and a cat and many people quite naturally turned to her. There was always something brewing on the Schmidmeister's stove; it was a place to sober up in the early morning hours while others came with clothes to mend, laundry to dry, or simply to have a chat. Holes in a curtain testify to visits from Carlotta Stocker who used to stop at the kitchen window gesturing with her cigarette. Maya gave Mattioli's sons lessons in English and French. She in turn could count on help from neighbors when Bert had to be calmed down and taken home. Otto Teucher's fatherly persuasion rarely failed to do the trick.

The spirit of renewal at Wuhrstrasse lasted into the 1970s, invigorated by many new residents and changing dynamics. Professional recognition went hand-in-hand with fiercely self-assertive players. Otto Müller and Trudi Demut were linchpins in this movement in which discipline did not always prevail over bacchanalia. Turbulent times were ensured by the notoriously wanton bravado of Friedrich Kuhn. His studio became the hub of a hodgepodge collection of people united in their disdain of the bourgeoisie. Alongside René Ed. Brauchli—he had already shared various studios with Kuhn and was soon to join the cooperative—habitués included the painters Muz Zeier, Alex Sadkowsky, Philipp Schibig and Fred E. Knecht, publisher and writer Silvio Baviera, filmmaker Georg Radanowicz, writer Paul Nizon, and others such as Tino, a leader in the Hells Angels. Nizon, who had taken stock of cultural life in Zurich in his *Zürcher Almanach* of 1968, became the most important connection for several Wuhrstrasse artists. Essential and enduring support also came from another frequent guest, the art critic Fritz Billeter.

Friedrich Kuhn, fierce and sensitive: he was admired for being unsparing to the point of self-destruction and he was loved for his childlike delight in play. Silvio Mattioli sat on his shoulders while he pedaled around Demut's studio on a bicycle without bumping into any of the fragile sculptures. The bicycle subsequently underwent plastic treatment and was transformed into a refined sculpture; unfortunately, its owner was not amused. Gatherings were not restricted to excesses drenched in alcohol. When Kuhn couldn't manage to finish his paintings for the Expo 64, Müller, Demut, and Mattioli rose to the occasion, completing them under his guidance the night before they were transported to Lausanne. Spotaneous help of that kind was nothing new. Otto Müller himself was once on the receiving end. His granite *Kuh mit Kälblein* (Cow with Calf) of 1953, intended for the Friesenberg schoolhouse, remained unfinished for years. When the city of Zurich finally put it up anyway, Mattioli joined him on site to help finish the work. The climate was so icy cold there that the two sculptors dubbed the schoolhouse "Alaska."

Carlotta Stocker, also a legendary figure, much admired or at least respected, died the same year as Kuhn—in 1972. Even the most successful male colleagues accepted the fact that she was their equal. Under the spell of Picasso and Matisse, she remained faithful to classical painting. The intensity with which she lived and painted was incredible, as was the freedom with which she carved an independent path of her own. Constantly entangled in love affairs, she claimed the right to determine her own life as a woman long before that right was propagated by the women's movement. Among the men she introduced to Wuhrstrasse, musician and composer Ermano Maggini made the most enduring impression on the other members of the cooperative.

Protagonists of the '68 movement found not only appreciative mothers and fathers at Wuhrstrasse but also live role models and active support, once again and most particularly in and from Otto Müller and Trudi Demut, who were lifelong champions of socialism and greatly esteemed the Marxist philosopher and art historian Konrad Farner. Remo Roth joined the cooperative in 1973; he was a member of the Gewerkschaft Kultur, Erziehung und Wissenschaft (GKEW, Union of Culture, Education, and Science) and of the Produzentengalerie, where

1   Silvio Mattioli welding his iron sculpture, *Stele*, 1962

2   Silvio Mattioli's courtyard workshop with the iron sculptures *Ikarus, Chimäre II*, and *Hahn*, 1962

3   Silvio Mattioli with *Stele* and *Chimäre II*, courtyard workshop, 1962

4   Silvio Mattioli with *Chimäre III*, courtyard workshop, 1961

Silvio Mattioli's courtyard workshop with iron sculpture
Lebensbaum, 1964

In Trudi Demut's studio, 1985

Demut and Müller also exhibited their work. Hansjörg Mattmüller moved in at the same time and threw a party that is said to have lasted an entire week. He cofounded the F+F Art School, which was also a product of the '68 movement.

When the Painters and Sculptors Building Cooperative Zurich celebrated its 25th anniversary in 1978 with an exhibition in the lobby of the Kunsthaus, the cooperative was in the best of health though decidedly more settled. Kuhn and Stocker had already joined the "ancestral gallery," while a number of younger members had moved in, among them the sculptor Ruedi Gregor, the painter Franz Grossert y Cañameras, and printmaker/painter Werner W. Wyss.

The 1980s were relatively quiet at Wuhrstrasse. The surviving original guard, engrossed in their work, hardly noticed how things were changing around them. Short-term residents also played a role, such as painter and engraver Peter Stiefel, and Klaudia Schifferle, who skyrocketed to fame with the paintings she presented at the 1982 *documenta*.

However, the idea of Wuhrstrasse as an organic community still had traction, as illustrated by René Ed. Brauchli's 1988 paraphrase of Courbet's *Atelier*, a monumental painting in which the famous allegory, set in his own studio at Wuhrstrasse, pictures artists from the cooperative as well as associated friends and allies.

After the death of Otto Müller in 1993, an almost eerie quiet followed at Wuhrstrasse. Trudi Demut's studio had been the cooperative's salon for decades; now it opened only rarely. Müller's partner in life and art devoted herself to his estate, while simultaneously creating a late work, which is now gradually coming into its own.

Edi Hebeisen, one of the few sculptors who still practice traditional stone carving, took over Müller's studio and workplace. Unlike Müller, who once had to put a stop to Mattioli's exuberant expansion, he no longer has to defend his territory. With no neighborly interference, Pietro Mattioli, William Lutz, and Urs Frei, the last to move in, work in almost monastic seclusion and in close association with the current art scene.

Pietro Mattioli took over Trudi Demut's studio after she died. In the course of almost fifty years, it had turned into a rampant universe, which he thoughtfully unburdened from all extraneous elements. His personal aesthetic needs are also an expression of the respect shown by the latest Wuhrstrassegeneration for Ernst Gisel's architecture. Silvio Mattioli's son has presided over the cooperative since 2002 and is perhaps even more of a purist regarding the building than Vivarelli and Teucher, who consistently opposed insensitive renovations.

Despite the continuing demand for affordable studios aggravated by minimal turnover in the cooperative, the Wuhrstrasse has remained the only address of this artists' building cooperative. For years, the board tried to find additional land, and plans had even been made for a larger project that would accommodate musicians, painters, and writers, but it proved too costly. The cooperative at the end of the 1960s may no longer have had the thrust and energy that gave birth to the original project.

POSTSCRIPT 2020: A SUCCESS STORY

Things have quieted down at Wuhrstrasse 8/10. Since Edi Hebeisen's early death in 2012, there is no one who works with stone anymore in this artists' cooperative, let alone iron. Art production has moved indoors and largely become dematerialized. The once so typical sculptor's workplaces are now courtyards, which, oddly enough, seem much smaller than in the days when they accommodated the making of sculptures weighing several tons.

Soon seventy years old, the Painters and Sculptors Building Cooperative Zurich represents a unique success story. The founders—a parthengenesis, as was usual at the time—would be most surprised to see the perfect condition of their colony today. The founding trio Otto Müller, Otto Teucher, and Max Truninger would have every reason to delight in the respectful cultivation of their heritage. Under the leadership of president Pietro Mattioli, the cooperative has seen substantial renovation over the past ten years with great care taken to preserve Ernst Gisel's architecture. What's more, not only the location but also the spirit of this visibly rejuvenated artists' colony lives on.

As before, a diversity of approaches is still united here—quiet creators and restless spirits, some well-established, others lesser-known. Fields of endeavor have also changed with the advent of new and younger artists. Traditional sculpture has given way to photography (Andrea Gohl, Pietro Mattioli, Caroline Palla) and video (Zilla Leutenegger, Veronika Spierenburg). For the most part, the artists work in several fields. The embrace of new media and interdisciplinary initiatives is largely indebted to Hansjörg Mattmüller, teacher at the F+F, who confronted the old guard at the end of the 1970s with the already long-familiar, expanded concept of art. In the wake of this reorientation, artist and draftswoman Valeria Stefané-Klausmann and her husband, cameraman Rainer Klausmann were welcomed into the cooperative. At about the same time, painter Doris Michel and self-taught sculptor Doris Dedual moved in as well.

In Urs Frei's work, painting, sculpture, and installation are inextricably intertwined, while Andreas Dobler still makes traditional paintings. William Lutz has remained faithful to the time-honored genres of drawings and prints. In contrast, Zilla Leutenegger ventures into all conceivable disciplines, with drawing playing a central role, for instance, integrated into videos, on paper as sgraffito, or in monotypes. Luigi Archetti also takes an interdisciplinary approach, working intensely with sounds and juxtaposing the world of sound with his visual output. Stefan Burger and Pietro Mattioli, both trained as photographers, produce primarily conceptual work, repeatedly in concert with the contingencies of space. A series of glazed ceramics in different colors pay tribute to Gisel's architecture, not only demonstrating Mattioli's sensitivity to materials but also his allegiance to the cooperative in which he grew up. No one is as knowledgeable as he is about its history and with it, the history of art in Zurich over the past seventy years. Patricia Bucher, the youngest member of the cooperative, also crosses boundaries, combining her conceptual and often architecturally related work with handmade picture supports, in particular weaving.

The first generation of artists at the cooperative did not restrict themselves to one specific genre, either. The sculptor Trudi Demut, a longtime pillar of this community, also painted, made installations, and increasingly found pleasure in using "low-class" materials. The famous photographer Jakob Tuggener, one of the first members of the cooperative, almost moved in himself, and there are still external members today, currently Remo Roth, Andrea Thal, and Mirjam Wirz.

The most striking change to be observed at Wuhrstrasse is how the artists see themselves. They have become more flexible, more internationally oriented, and correspondingly less sedentary. This naturally affects the life of the community. People have become more individualistic and rarely meet spontaneously. Being less close-knit also means less conflict. Exchange among individuals has to be organized, as in the summer party of 2019 where musicians Archetti and Dobler made music together for the first time.

Who knows, maybe a second Wuhrstrasse may come about someday after all. Whatever the case, the old project of another cooperative artists' colony is still on the table—at least as a utopia.

This article was first published in the 2003 anniversary publication *50 Jahre Baugenossenschaft Maler und Bildhauer Wuhrstrasse 8/10*. It is reprinted here with a postscript.

Sculptor and draftsman Karl Hebeisen's studio and outdoor workshop, 2008

1	Otto Müller's courtyard workshop, (left to right) unidentified, Friedrich Kuhn, Trudi Demut, Otto Müller, c. 1960

2	Friedrich Kuhn in his studio, 1960

3	Work place Silvio Mattioli with unfinished iron sculpture *Kreuzweg* for the Kloster zum guten Hirten, a monastery in Altstätten/SG, 1966

1 Otto Müller's courtyard workshop, c. 1960

2 Otto Morach's studio with paintings from 1912 to 1917, c. 1965

3 Otto Morach in his studio, next to a sculpture by Hermana Morach-Sjövall and paintings from the 1910s and 1920s, c. 1965

Ueber genossenschaftliches Denken

Ein Beitrag zur 19. Generalversammlung der Genossenschaft Maler und Bildhauer Zürich, am 28. Mai 1970, von Otto Müller.

Wer fähig wäre, jeden Tag alles in Frage zu ziehen um alles immer wieder neu zu sehen und neu zu erleben, würde wohl kaum dem fast unausbleiblichen Phänomen der Erstarrung anheimfallen, einer Gefahr, der fast alle menschlichen Einrichtungen bei langem Gebrauch ausgesetzt sind. Deshalb ist es wichtig, über eine Institution, wie unsere Genossenschaft es ist, von Zeit zu Zeit nachzudenken und zu rekapitulieren, was eine Genossenschaft eigentlich ist und worauf es ankommt, um ihr einen sinnvollen Bestand zu sichern; sich wieder einmal vor Augen zu führen, dass eine Genossenschaft nichts ist, das einfach gegeben und selbstverständlich wäre, dass vielmehr eine Absicht und ein Wille zur Erreichung eines bestimmten Zieles dahinter steht. In unserem Fall: das Wohnen und Arbeiten der Genossenschafter unter möglichst günstigen ökonomischen Verhältnissen in einer menschlich würdigen und angenehmen Atmosphäre. Doch ist zu bedenken: dass das nur realisiert werden kann, wo jeder Einzelne seine persönlichen Interessen dem Ganzen unterordnet, dass er in seinem Handeln das gemeinsame Ziel nie ausseracht lassen darf, ohne das Ganze zu gefährden, dass in einer Genossenschaft alle Mitglieder die gleichen Rechte haben, dass der Vorstand keine Privilegien besitzt und kein profitgieriger "Hausmeister" ist, sondern lediglich die laufenden Geschäfte zu behandeln und die Interessen der Genossenschafter nach innen und aussen zu wahren hat, dass er bereit ist, jederzeit Anregungen und konstruktive Vorschläge der Genossenschafter entgegen zu nehmen und dass man sollte erwarten dürfen, dass dort, wo Konflikte entstehen, jeder bereit und fähig wäre, die strittigen Fragen objektiv zu sehen und sachlich zu beurteilen und dass aus der Erkenntnis, dass man auf so engem Raum aufeinander angewiesen ist, wie etwa Astronauten in ihrer Kapsel, sich alles in einer höflichen und rücksichts- und vertrauensvollen Respektierung des Andern abspielte. So könnte eine Genossenschaft über ihren unmittelbaren Zweck hinaus Vorbild und Beispiel menschlichen Betragens und Zusammenlebens sein und ein bescheidener Anfang und Beitrag zu einer erstrebenswerten Ordnung für unsere ganze Welt.

———

120

Otto Morach in his studio, c. 1955

THE STUDIO
AS MYTH
AND VIBRANT
PRESENT

STEFAN ZWEIFEL

Implicit in each studio is an ideology… So we can "read" studios as texts that are as revelatory in their way as artworks themselves.—Brian O'Doherty

The myth of the studio[1] as house and home to individual genius, as the artist's second skin or even as a work of art in its own right beyond the maker's death—embodied, indeed epitomized by Alberto Giacometti in Paris, as illustrated by doors and plaster fragments from the studio, exhibited at the Fondation Giacometti in Paris (behind glass as if they were sacred relics)—that myth came under assault in the serial form of studios introduced, for example, by the Bauhaus[2] and built at Wuhrstrasse in Zurich.

The notion of the artist as a craftsperson in a kind of manufactory, whose structure is not individual but rather serial, was reinforced at the time by the political strategy of socially integrating the wild "bohemian" as a valuable worker in "spick-and-span studios"[3]—thus successfully persuading the Zurich City Council in 1952 to grant the Baugenossenschaft Maler und Bildhauer Zürich (the Painters and Sculptors Building Cooperative Zurich) a mortgage on their property.[4] In the course of Wuhrstrasse's history, the glorification of the studio was naturally and subversively undermined—not least thanks to Friedrich Kuhn. In his essay of 1948, "Wer soll Künstlerateliers bauen?" (Who should build artists' studios?), Alfred Roth, mentor to Ernst Gisel and godfather, so to speak, of this experiment, describes the studio as follows: "It is a sacred place, where the noblest and most sublime endeavors a creative person can produce come to fruition."[5] This exalted ideal lost some of its shine in the course of dialectical tension between political (like-minded) opinion and artistic self-realization. René Ed. Brauchli's painting *Das Atelier* (The Studio, 1988)—to which we will return—also pictures a thoroughly ruptured communal atmosphere. At Wuhrstrasse, various means of escaping the iron grip of such idealizations inevitably emerged, carving paths to a vibrant present.

THE STUDIO AS COUNTER-WORLD

Since the nineteenth century, the artist has been envisioned in his studio in heroic hyperbole. A workshop in which, like the Greek god Hephaestus, he forges red hot primordial matter into new creations, into utopian alternatives to bourgeois society, the sound of which swells more and more, decade by decade, all around the studio: a flood of rampant consumerism whose breakers were, as Gustav Flaubert put it, an "ocean of shit" battering his "ivory tower" so that the artist had to build the dams and walls of the studio higher and higher to protect himself from being consumed by healthy common sense—and then, like Flaubert with his novel *Bouvard et Pécuchet* (1881), "tossing a few boxes of shit onto the heads" of the bourgeoisie.

This dialectic of the godlike individual in his ivory tower and the conformist masses outside gradually led to the studio becoming an increasingly heterotopian[6] counter-site, a haven for a different life where the only thing that matters is the unfolding of the ultimate self in the act of creation. Of course, certain painters like Hans Makart gratified the voyeuristic instinct of the bourgeoisie, permitting them an occasional glimpse of this seedbed of novelty, preferably on a comfortable Sunday afternoon. But for the most part, artists guarded the privilege of picturing their studios as they saw fit or having a colleague paint portraits of them in the studio. Later, as in Giacometti's case, photographers came flocking to render their own version of the artist as the divine forger of aesthetic weapons and projectiles. Setting the stage and pace ahead of them all was Brassaï with his reportage from the studios of Henri Matisse, Pablo Picasso, and Giacometti.[7]

The seclusion of these counter-worlds in white-walled ivory towers,[8] the secularized form of the monastic cell, would ultimately define the White

---

1 Ina Conzen, ed., *Mythos Atelier—von Spitzweg bis Picasso, von Giacometti bis Naumann*, exh. cat., Hirmer, Munich, 2012.
2 Cf. Masters' houses by Walter Gropius built in Dessau in 1925/26.
3 Pietro Mattioli, ed., *50 Jahre Baugenossenschaft Maler und Bildhauer Wuhrstrasse 8/10*, self-published, Zurich, 2003, p. 8.
4 Ibid., pp. 23f.
5 Ibid., p. 27.
6 In his lecture "Des espaces autres," Michel Foucault applies the term heterotopia to museums as well as gardens, but does not mention the artist's studio. Michel Foucault, *Dits et Ecrits II*, Gallimard, Paris, 2001, p. 1571.
7 Cf. Mary Bergstein, "The Artist in His Studio: Photography, Art, and the Masculine Mystique," in idem, Michelle Grabner, eds., *The Studio Reader*, University of Chicago Press, Chicago/London, 2010.

Cube,[9] which hotwired art and commerce as the transit gateway between studio and collector's flat.[10] To this day, photographs of studios in catalogues still function as stamps of authenticity.[11] The modern myth of the "studio" has largely been shaped by the paradigm of Giacometti's studio in Paris.

GIACOMETTI'S STUDIO AS THE COSMOS OF CREATION

The artist shapes the microcosm in his studio just as the Maker shapes the amorphous matter of the macrocosm. The studio resembles an echo chamber of the universe. As the ancient philosopher Lucretius explained in his didactic poem *De rerum natura,* elementary atoms once plunged in free fall through the infinite funnel of the universe, but *clinamen,* that is, random deviations, caused the triangular and quadrangular molecules to swerve away from their perpendicular fall and become entangled in ever larger configurations, living beings but incapable of life because these primordial monsters had neither womb nor phallus for reproduction; and so these creatures expired in the infinity of time until new beings capable of reproduction emerged. An endless round of creations, emerging and fading in the fascinating "innocence of becoming," as Friedrich Nietzsche once said.

And wasn't Giacometti's studio a microcosm of this kind, a small rendition of these erupting and disappearing worlds? Didn't the structures of his phantasms keep getting enmeshed in new entities, as in his *Femme en forme d'araignée* (1929), savagely ensnared in a desperate, violent act of love, before the single limbs dismembered by Dionysian lust—a single hand, like *La main* (1947) with fingers splayed in abject fear, death-rattling mouths and phallic noses—circled in the funnel of the studio round the sculpture *La Jambe* (1958)?[12]

So, too, do the successful creations stand on pedestals in the uterus of the usually male creator, while on the edges and walls the bungled creations gradually founder and sink in the dust and debris on the floor, while Giacometti's trousers, spattered with plaster, as glimpsed, for example, in photographs by Ernst Scheidegger, actually serve as the pedestal of the artist as statue.

Despite what Jean Genet or Jean-Paul Sartre, Michel Leiris or James Lord have to say, a modicum of the mystery remains unexplained: the ashes of the days, the dust of the plaster, scattered on the floor of the studio, piling higher and higher. The "leavings" of work in the service of art, *déjet,* thrown away. In the process, the studio itself becomes a kind of "subjectile,"[13] a "ground" that underlies painting beyond subject and object and that the writer Antonin Artaud abused by burning holes into it and bruising it with his pencil in order to give birth to new forms that defy standardization. So the studio can also be seen as a "ground" under statues of men and women rising erect only to go limp and flaccid again: "In this studio, a person dies slowly, self-consumed and transformed into goddesses before our eyes."[14]

The studio as both grave and womb. Even for Alberto the child, a cave dug into the snow in Bergell—he would later call it "Isba," a Siberian hut—was a womb. So it is not surprising that, when he signed the lease for his studio on December 1, 1926, he would never, with near superstitious tenacity, leave it again until his death forty years later. He pictured it in two drawings of 1932 before opening it up to photographers and thus to the outside world, which was permitted to view this singular place for the first time in Brassaï's photograph. This glorification culminated in 1972 when part of the wall was dismantled and moved to the Fondation Giacometti—a kind of mourning impressively described by Michel Leiris.[15] Nonetheless, one must not forget that this studio was part of a row of studios, or rather workshops,[16] and as singular as it might have been alongside its neighbors, one could envision it in a row of other related studios and imagine them, liberated from time and space, stretching out next to and above each other at Wuhrstrasse.

In his essay, "Die weisse Ausstellungswand—zur Vorgeschichte des 'white cube,'" Walter Grasskamp traces the triumphant crusade of the white wall to exhibitions of the Wiener Secession shortly after the turn of the century, Klimt's representation at the Venice Biennale of 1910, or the Sonderbund exhibition of 1912 in Cologne. In *Weiss,* eds. Wolfgang Ullrich, Juliane Vogel, S. Fischer Verlag, Frankfurt a.M., 2002, pp. 29–62. The journal *Werk,* 1 (1955), p. 16, writes about Wuhrstrasse: "The walls inside have not been plastered either and have been painted white."

Brian O'Doherty analyzes this dialectic *Atelier und Galerie / Studio and Cube,* Merve Verlag, Berlin 2012. This is the source of our motto as well.

10 Or as Brian O'Doherty puts it: "The classic modernist gallery is the limbo between studio and living room." See his seminal essay *Inside the White Cube,* The Lapis Press, San Francisco, 1986, p. 76.

11 According to Wolfgang Ullrich in his polemic essay "'Erwin anrufen'—oder: Wie wird künstlerische Kreativität mitgeteilt," in idem, *Gesucht: Kunst! Phantombild eines Jokers,* Wagenbach, Berlin 2007. And regarding the studio visits of collectors like Christian Flick, he opines that closeness to creativity is their favorite status symbol, p. 141.

12 When André Breton asked Giacometti what a studio was, he replied: "My two feet." In: Alberto Giacometti, *Ecrits,* Editions Hermann, Paris, 1997, p. 504.

13 Jacques Derrida, "To Unsense the Subjectile," in idem, Paule Thévenin, *The secret art of Antonin Artaud,* transl. Mary Ann Caws, MIT Press, Massachusetts, 1998.

14 Jean Genet, *l'atelier d'alberto giacometti,* L'Arbalète, Paris, 1958, n.p.

15 Michel Leiris, "Andere Zeit, andere Spuren ..." in *Wege zu Giacometti,* eds. Louis Aragon, et al., Matthes & Seitz, Munich, 1987, pp. 229–232ff.

16 The plan of the studio is reproduced in *L'atelier d'Alberto Giacometti,* Éditions du Centre Pompidou, Paris, 2008, p. 21. In the 1930s, Alberto rented a studio across the way for his brother Diego and in 1957 the second one for himself.

1   In Trudi Demut's studio, c. 1958

2   In Trudi Demut's studio, 1950s

3   Trudi Demut working on the bronze sculpture *Figur I*, Wuhrstrasse courtyard workshop, 1965

In Trudi Demuth's studio, c. 1960

PARALLEL WORLDS: ANDREAS WALSER'S "DRUNKEN BOAT"

Like Giacometti, 1920s Paris attracted another young artist from the Grisons, Andreas Walser. He, too, immersed himself in this rhizomatous counter-world of studios in Montmartre and Montparnasse, described as follows by Annemarie Schwarzenbach: "People rarely worked, enjoying themselves at studio parties, in bars and dance locales, [...] they sat around in dirty studios and made little pancakes on paraffin cookers that were called crêpe suzettes and tasted like burnt sugar. The atmosphere exuded the aging magic of bohemian and romantic life."[17]

In Andreas Walser's case—he snorted cocaine with Klaus Mann, who was also a friend of Schwarzenbach—it was rather more a black romanticism: feverish and wasted, Walser spent more and more time in his studio, darkening it like van Gogh did.[18] Protected and advised by his fatherly friend Ernst Ludwig Kirchner, he tried to find true form, turning first to Alberto Savinio, then to Jean Cocteau, and later coming to terms with his impressions after visiting Picasso's studio.[19] Dispirited, he noted:

> "young artists—don't listen
> to the voices of the great geniuses.
> they kill us.
> invent—? we have come
> too late for that"[20]

Despite this insight, he must have been devastated by Kirchner's reproach in March 1930: "When will you get around to making genuine Walsers?"[21] And equally by Kirchner's reference to the "interesting sculpture"[22] by Alberto Giacometti, which had been reproduced in Georges Bataille's journal *Documents*. That hit hard, even more so since he had fallen in love with Bruno Giacometti: "I suffered pain and agony for over a year because of him. All of my passion, so early erupted, concentrated on him!—Bruno Giacometti! He is gloriously beautiful [...] one cannot write everything [...] then everything broke down because of Bruno's cruelty."[23]

Lonely, largely unsuccessful and wasted, he roamed the streets of Paris: "sometimes/I am afraid/to go home/so late/so alone at night."[24] He fought his fear with morphine and opium. After spending "3 days unconscious in bed," he painted *Abstraction* with the pastose inscription *MORPHINE*, while "my veins [look] pitch black."[25] He barricaded himself inside his "Studio Fear" with increasing intensity. He lived there as if in a womb. The symbiosis was even more extreme than in Giacometti's case. He practically began drinking the studio!

Frenzy starts racing about in his rooms when he not only sniffs the scent of oil paints, varnish, and oranges but also begins drinking ink and toxic "paint oils."[26] His studio is completely transformed into Rimbaud's "drunken boat." And as an intoxicated "ject," as a "river," Walser melts stroke by stroke, swallow by swallow, into this paint oil, into the pigments on his palette. It is a fitting end that this studio was washed away after he died, a "drunken boat," torn down and largely forgotten, like his oeuvre.

AN IMAGINARY WUHRSTRASSE BEYOND SPACE AND TIME

This singular studio, beyond space and time, could be linked in a serial chain along with Francis Bacon's studio or with Friedrich Kuhn's studio at Wuhrstrasse.

In contrast to Carlotta Stocker's and Carlo Vivarelli's tidy studios, Friedrich Kuhn's room, pictured in photographs and in H.R. Giger's *Painting*, looks like a greedy devouring maw, as if Georg Radanowicz had just shot his film *Pic-Nic* (1967) in it, as if Kuhn's gluttonous Gargantuan meal laid out in the film were the reverse shot of the frugal Protestant table seen in photographs of the inauguration at Wuhrstrasse in 1953.

---

17 Annemarie Schwarzenbach, *Freunde um Bernhard*, Amalthea-Verlag, Zurich/Leipzig/Vienna, 1931, pp. 96f.
18 Andreas Walser to his brother Peter, Oct. 8, 1928 (unpublished).
19 Walser gave him the painting *Buste à la fenêtre* with the dedication: "à Pablo Picasso son petit élève Andréas Walser."
20 Translated from French to German (SZ) to English (CS) after the largely unpublished studies for *Le Balcon*.
21 Kirchner to Walser, no date (March 3, 1930).
22 Ibid.
23 Walser to Bärby Hunger, Chur, Feb. 2, 1928.
24 Andreas Walser, *Le Balcon*.
25 Walser to Bärby Hunger, May 4, 1929.
26 Ibid.

But would the four artists—Giacometti, Walser, Bacon, Kuhn—united in one place have been able to tolerate the proximity of their excesses? Wouldn't Walser's grief upon the rebuff of Alberto's brother have been intolerably aggravated? And wouldn't Kuhn's gluttonous orgies have been insufferable for Alberto Giacometti, who ate practically nothing but bread with camembert? Wouldn't these excesses have neutralized and indeed canceled each other out?

Michael Peppiatt was well acquainted with Bacon's studio and devoted an entire volume to Giacometti's studio. He "often wondered whether Bacon, who was otherwise so immaculate in appearance and manner, hadn't modelled his chaotic studio—and hence part of his 'myth'—after Giacometti's."[27] Whatever the case, a photograph of Giacometti himself was found between magazines and postcards in one of Bacon's drawers. In physical proximity, this "copy" would probably have been too obvious, and nobody is likely to be interested in staging assembly-line images of the artist as outlaw for the society of the spectacle.

POST-STUDIO PRACTICE

While new artists moved into the classical studios at Wuhrstrasse in the course of the 1970s, their choice had already become curiously outmoded. John Baldessari was teaching a Post-Studio art class at Cal Arts at the time although he himself maintained several studios—office studio, print studio, and main Venice studio—ironically confessing, "God forbid that it leaked out that I had a studio."[28] The skeptical take on traditional studios culminated in Daniel Buren's essay, "The Function of the Studio"[29] of 1971. He analyzed the contradiction of producing works in a studio that ultimately retain their true form only in situ, before they are transferred to a gallery, a White Cube that is necessarily an avatar.

And so, in the 1970s, the physiognomy of the studio changed. Beuys advanced the philosophy of producing "social sculptures" in a social context and installed an "office" at *documenta 5* 1972, thereby transforming art into discourse. At the same time, performance conquered all kinds of spaces, including the street outside.

On the other hand, the studio itself became a work of art, replete with a readymade[30] in the form of the artist himself—as when Bruce Nauman presented himself in his *Portrait of the Artist as Fountain*, 1966. Subsequently, he presented the studio as subject matter most impressively in his video projection of 2002, *Mapping the Studio/Fat Chance John Cage*. The video begins just as Nauman leaves the studio and us with a picture of an empty room populated by the cat, mice, and nocturnal white sound. The title refers to the striking description of Cage's studio: "You know, when you enter your studio, everyone is there, the people in your life, other artists, the old masters, everyone. And as you work they leave, one by one. And if it is a really good working day, well, you leave too."

Nonetheless the venerable myth of the studio still persists: curtain raiser of the exhibition *Mapping the Studio. Artists from the François Pinault Collection* at the 2009 Venice Biennale consisted of fifty photographs of artists' studios.

Several exhibitions in 2010 and *The Studio Reader* outline the historical context of the studio. Astonishingly, none of the texts, books, and exhibitions have ever inquired into the specific nature of a group of studios in one place—except for historical entities, which emerged at random, like the *Bateau-Lavoir*, where artists like Picasso and writers like Max Jacob launched cubism, or *La Ruche*, the Parisian beehive that enjoyed its heyday in the 1920s thanks to Marc Chagall, Amadeo Modigliani, and Constantin Brancusi.[31] It is the concentration of such diverse artists that makes the model of Wuhrstrasse so fascinating.

Michael Peppiatt, *in giacometti's stu-* Yale University Press, New Haven, CT, 2010, p. 17. on's studio was moved from 7 Reece Mews in South sington to the Hugh Lane Gallery, where it has been on since 2001.

Mary Jane Jacob, Michelle Grabner, *The Studio Reader: On the Space of Artists*, University of Chicago Press, 2010, p. 31.

Daniel Buren, "The Function of the Studio," transl. Thomas Repensek, in *October*, Vol. 10 (Autumn, 1979), pp. 51–58.

30 Let it be said, however, that Marcel Duchamp had a secret studio in which he worked on *Etant donnés*. It was not to be revealed until after his death and undermines the myth of the conceptual artist without a fixed room.

31 Blaise Cendrars describes this artists' colony in a poem of 1913 as follows:
"The Beehive
Stairways, doors, stairways
And his door opens like a newspaper
Covered with visiting cards
Then it closes.
Disorder, total disorder
Photographs of Léger, photographs of Tobeen, which you don't see
And on the back
Frantic works
Sketches, drawings, frantic works
And paintings …
Empty bottles"
In: Blaise Cendrars, *Complete Poems*, transl. Ron Padgett, University of California Press, 1993, p. 61.

In Friedrich Kuhn's studio, (left to right) unidentified guitar player, Philipp Schibig, Friedrich Kuhn, Muz Zeier (standing), Nicolas Bregenzer, Silvio R. Baviera, René Ed. Brauchli, Ernst Bucher (in the foreground), c. 1969

RENÉ ED. BRAUCHLI: *DAS ATELIER* (1988)

The dream that Alfred Roth dreamt of an artists' colony in the spirit of the Bauhaus has of course eroded. Representatives of "mini worlds of madness" were now working side-by-side with constructivists like Carlo Vivarelli, and soon afterwards Claudia Schifferle, one of the so-called "wild ones," came along. History did not bow to a serial version of creation—luckily.

In the mid-nineteenth century, in his monumental painting *The Artist's Studio*[32] (1854/55), conceived as a manifesto, Courbet had already depicted the diverse, contradictory, and heteroclitic nature of the studio. His "allegory of reality" shows the painter next to a nude model, a dog (primal nature) and a child (the future), in front of an easel with blue sky bursting into the middle of the studio. To the left, Courbet assembled the social contradictions of his day, among them Napoleon III next to a Jew; to the right stand those united in the artistic battle against the bourgeoisie, first and foremost Charles Baudelaire, exponent of Realism and precursor of Impressionism.

René Ed. Brauchli's version of *The Studio* at Wuhrstrasse (1988) (see pp. 170–171) is similarly heteroclitic. Instead of Napoleon III, Federal Councilor Elisabeth Kopp, the adversary in Brauchli's version, is seen on a TV screen with a drug addict lying on the floor in front of her. Allies, like Otto Müller and Trudi Demut, stand close together, but eyed from a critical distance by Paul Nizon, who was more interested in Friedrich Kuhn's mini madness in the wake of surrealism and described his work as follows:

"It comes to flourishing outgrowths and eloquent things, to monstrously heaped furnishings, whose architecture and sculptural shape are immersed in a jungle of color—and drown in inimitable beauty. Actually, he always manages to do the magic trick of turning rubbish into beauty."[33] Nizon proceeds to picture the artist as an outlaw, who takes the "perspective of a clochard" in questioning "our welfare-state existence" and therefore naturally also Alfred Roth's statement quoted at the outset.

"IDIORHYTHMIA" AS UTOPIA

"Comment vivre ensemble?"—"How to live together?" Roland Barthes asked himself this question in his penultimate lecture.[34] He was still living with his mother in an apartment near the Place St-Sulpice in Paris. Did he sense that his mother would soon die and bring an end to their curious symbiosis? That she would no longer supply him with baskets full of mail, books, and food through a trapdoor in the floor of his room?

How to live together in a different, new community? How could he defend his own life rhythm, his "idiorhythm," against the pressures of community life? He remembers the monastery on the mountain of Athos in Greece, where eccentric hermits live on the steep slopes, meeting only occasionally—it would be conceivable to live together that way in a group of three to eight people, who wander about at will following their own daily "idiorhythm," with the rhythmic vibrations ideally complementing each other and coming together in harmony.

"Comment vivre ensemble" sets in where Barthes's fragments about a twosome talking of love end. In real life, he was fond of but also repelled by "the clique" (grouped around Philippe Sollers and Julia Kristeva). He avoided all gatherings, preferring to meet friends one at a time rather than too many "togethered." In-difference always dominates the group; only on a one-to-one basis can the play of difference be given free rein.

"I want to live on the basis of nuance." This is what Barthes answered when asked how he wants to act in the face of current ideological and intellectual debate. He wanted to retreat into a nonideological, "neutral" space. Neutrality undermines paradigm. It is neither true nor false; it says neither yes or

---

32 Werner Hofmann, *Das Atelier—Courbets Jahrhundertbild*, C.H. Beck, Munich, 2010.
33 Paul Nizon, "Zürcher Schule der kleinen Wahnwelt," in *Zürcher Almanach*, Benziger Verlag, Zurich/Cologne/Einsiedeln, 1968.
34 Roland Barthes, *Comment vivre ensemble—Cours et séminaires au Collège de France (1976–1977)*. Sous la direction d'Eric Marty, texte établi, annoté et présenté par Claude Coste, Editions du Seuil/IMEC, Paris, 2002.

Carlotta Stocker in her studio, 1966

Otto Teucher in his studio, behind him a model for a mural, late 1960s

no but rather fades into the infinitesimal dust of perception: in the "teaism" of Taoism, when the tea is simmering and the bubbles appear as fish eyes in a brook that slowly, slowly becomes a burbling spring again, a self-birth.

In the echo chamber of almost fictional fragments, Barthes gazes out at the sea from the terrace of the Athos monastery, where banks of male and female fish float superimposed, fertilizing each other in the depths, a bouquet of flowers in front of the window, lying in bed and seen in feverish fatigue as the eternal promise of utopian happiness, while waiting, like Proust's protagonist Marcel, for his mother's kiss of redemption. After her death, the utopia of living together becomes an atopy for Barthes—placeless, defined only in the imaginary. But by 1970 popular culture had already produced a model of how idiorhythms can unfold in a community: Barbapapa and his utopian house.

BARBAPAPAMAMAHOUSE

Wuhrstrasse is also reminiscent of this utopian site. The structure of Ernst Gisel's building recalls the house Barbapapa built with his family on the outskirts of the city after they had been evicted from an old villa that had to make way for concrete blocks of residential cells. Barbapapa and his family are squeezed into one of the cells but then escape onto a hill outside the city. They ward off the onslaught of excavators and wrecking balls with bombs of sticky marmalade and build their dream house, adding one round room after the other.

Barbapapa and Barbamama lie in bed and have Barbabelle serve them something to drink, music comes out of the flute-shaped chimneys of Barbalala's room, while sweaty Barbabravo is busy lifting weights and Barbabright is covering the walls of his room with mathematical formulas, as if it were the second floor of the building Gilles Deleuze described in his study of the Baroque.[35] Yes, this house is ultimately Baroque: each individual is free to unfold within it. And in the midst of it all, Barbabeau's studio. The painter feels comfortable there, at liberty to develop within the family fold, unfettered by the stranglehold of capital.

A heterogeneous array of artists is similarly disrupting the modernist unity once conceived for the studios and flats at Wuhrstrasse, as shown in the insert of Zara Pfeifer's photographs.

Wuhrstrasse now awaits a congenial writer to map its inner life as Georges Perec once did with such verve in his experimental novel, *Life: A User's Manual*.[36] He describes a block of flats in Paris at 8 p.m. on June 23, 1975 in ninety-nine chapters, prefacing them with a self-imposed set of rules: every chapter has to mention forty-two terms that he had previously distributed mathematically—colors, furniture, writers, and works of art. We jump from chapter to chapter, from room to room, while the plot that has come to a halt on this evening gradually begins to unravel. The traces of an art project trail from room to room, from the cellar to the attic by elevator. The eccentric millionaire Bartlebooth painted 500 ports the world over in 500 aquarelles, a project meant to leave no trace behind. He gave them to Gaspard Winckler, a master puzzle maker, who cuts up the aquarelles, for Bartlebooth to put them together again. In the end, dipped into the water of forgetting and pristine white again, they would each be lowered down again into the waters at their port of origin. But Bartlebooth, who has devoted his life to this work without work, dies over the last piece of the 439th puzzle, which does not have the missing shape of an X but rather a W…

Organic life trips up the concept; Wuhrstrasse has broken out of the historical concept into the wide-open present.

The solemn pathos that culminated in a speech by Otto Müller of 1970 during a meeting of Wuhrstrasse tenants has thus been unexpectedly fulfilled: "A modest beginning of a desirable order for the whole world." Perhaps, with Zara Pfeifer's photographs mounted on the wall above the desk, a writer should now pen a new novel: Wuhrstrasse at 8 p.m. on June 23, 2021. Title: *Studio. A User's Manual*.

Gilles Deleuze, *The Fold*, transl. Tom …ley, University of Minnesota Press, Minneapolis, 1993. …euze mentions that there was a "canvas diversified by …s" on the second floor of the Baroque building, with rows …umbers purling down, and refers to paintings by Raus- …nberg and Jackson Pollock.

36 Georges Perec, *Life: A User's Manual*, transl. David Bellos, Verba Mundi, 2009.

Freitag, 24. Februar 1978 — ZÜRI LEU — Seite 3

Ein Vierteljahrhundert Kunst an der Wuhrstrasse in Wiedikon: das Backsteinhaus von Architekt Ernst Gisel

Engagierte Kunst über Raum, Zeit und Mensch: Werner W. Wyss

Eine Ausstellung im Kunsthaus-Foyer dokumentiert das Gelingen eines einzigartigen Experimentes: die genossenschaftliche Selbsthilfe der «Künstler an der Wuhrstrasse».

Das Haus ihrer Träume

Im Foyer des Kunsthauses wird unter dem Titel «Künstler an der Wuhrstrasse» eine Art Rechenschaftsbericht über 25 Jahre «Baugenossenschaft Maler und Bildhauer an der Wuhrstrasse 8 und 10» gezeigt. Diese genossenschaftliche Selbsthilfe ist auch heute noch mustergültig und wegleitend. Leider hat diese Lösung des Atelierproblems bis heute keine Nachahmung gefunden.

Drei Künstler sind als die eigentlichen Initianten dieses Werkes anzusprechen: Der Maler *Max Truninger*, die Bildhauer *Otto Teucher* und *Otto Müller*. Diese drei haben nach vorausgegangenen jahrelangen Bemühungen, Sondierungen und Besprechungen, vielen Fehldispositionen und enttäuschten Hoffnungen im Jahre 1949 eine Baugenossenschaft gegründet.

Bildhauer Otto Müller erinnert sich heute: «In den vierziger Jahren, vor allem nach dem Zweiten Weltkrieg, wurden immer wieder Häuser, in denen sich Künstler mit grossem Einsatz und materiellem Aufwand provisorische Ateliers eingerichtet hatten, abgebrochen, so dass diese mit ihren Kunstwerken und ihren Siebensachen buchstäblich auf der Strasse standen. Die Verdienstmöglichkeiten der Künstler waren auch nicht rosig, grosse Aufträge waren rar, die Käufer blieben meist aus, und man hatte sich oft mit ausserkünstlerischen Erwerbsquellen behelfen müssen. Das war die Ausgangslage für die genossenschaftliche Selbsthilfe.»

Der Zweck der neuen Genossenschaft war die Beschaffung von Ateliers und Wohnraum für hauptberuflich arbeitende Künstler unter möglichst günstigen ökonomischen Verhältnissen in einer menschlich würdigen und angenehmen Atmosphäre.

Die Genossenschaft fand bald unter den Architekten einen Freund: *Ernst Gisel*. Dieser war den Initianten immer wieder mit gutem Rat behilflich. «Im unbedingten Vertrauen auf unser gestecktes Ziel und mit der Unterstützung wohlgesinnter, einflussreicher Leute sind wir langsam an die massgebenden Stellen gelangt und haben deren Interesse zu wecken vermocht. Und was wir früher kaum zu glauben wagten, hat sich endlich realisiert», meint heute Otto Müller.

Im Frühjahr 1952 hat der Stadtrat von Zürich mit der Genossenschaft einen Vertrag über die Abtretung eines Stückes Bauland von 1285 Quadratmeter an der Wuhrstrasse im Baurecht auf die Dauer von 80 Jahren gegen einen Baurechtszins von 3½ Prozent und über den Bau eines Atelier- und Wohnhauses mit 12 Ateliers und 8 Wohnungen nach Plänen von Architekt Ernst Gisel abgeschlossen.

Das Vorhaben konnte nur unter namhafter finanzieller Hilfe des Kantons und der Stadt Zürich durchgeführt werden. Die gesamte Bausumme betrug 463 000 Franken, wovon die Stadt die erste und die zweite Hypothek übernahm. Die Genossenschaft selbst konnte immerhin ein symbolisches Kapital von 28 000 Franken aufbringen. Mit dem Bau des Hauses wurde Mitte Juli 1952 begonnen. Im März 1953 konnten die Ateliers bezogen werden.

Max Truninger war der erste Präsident der Genossenschaft, er wurde abgelöst durch den heutigen Präsidenten Otto Teucher. Otto Müller blieb immer im Windschatten als Vizepräsident.

Als Voraussetzung zum besseren Erreichen des Zieles der Genossenschaft — das ungestörte und reibungslose Nebeneinanderschaffen und Nebeneinanderwohnen — wird jeder neue Mieter durch einige festgelegte Grundsätze über genossenschaftliches Denken darauf aufmerksam gemacht, dass das Ziel nur Wirklichkeit werden kann, wenn jeder einzelne seine persönlichen Interessen dem Ganzen unterordnet.

Heute ist die Künstlerkolonie Wuhrstrasse — ein Komplex von einem Dutzend Ateliers — eine Selbstverständlichkeit. Nach aussen hin hat sich nach einem anfänglichen Misstrauen und einer offensichtlichen Abneigung von seiten gewisser Nachbarn und Anwohner gegen dieses Künstlerhaus und seine Bewohner sehr bald ein gutnachbarliches, ja sogar freundschaftliches Verhältnis herausgebildet.

Die Ausstellung im Kunsthaus zeigt, dass das Haus auch heute noch ein Zentrum kreativen Schaffens ist und dass das gemeinsam angestrebte Ziel erreicht worden ist.

Alfred Messerli
Fotos: Willy Spiller

Will die neuesten Werke noch nicht zeigen: Trudi Demut

Der Bildhauer Otto Teucher, Gründer und heutiger Präsident

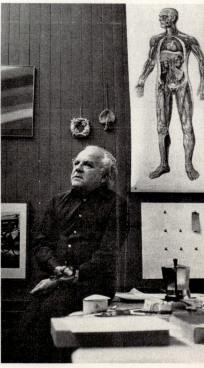

Ein Theoretiker der Kunst: Hansjörg Mattmüller (F+F)

René Brauchli:
Im Atelier den Kater Abraham

bei Schmerzen — schnell und lange wirksam
apodol®

Erol gegen **Haarausfall**
Das biologische Haarwasser — in jedem Fachgeschäft ab Fr. 6.—

Züri Leu, February 24, 1978

LIVING AND WORKING—ON THE NORMALIZATION OF ARTISTIC WORK

BURKHARD MELTZER

Artists live and work. This sentence, with corresponding place name, introduces the short text that accompanies practically every art exhibition, media release, or grant application. The information inevitably provokes geographical and cultural allocations: known or unknown, center or periphery, and sometimes several places—possibly as an indication of cosmopolitan mobility. In addition, the information seems to reassure a potential public: artists live and work, too. The matter-of-fact formulation is not much different from the description of any other occupation, and yet, no résumé for any other form of employment would ever begin by stating the location of one's life and work.

As mundane as this observation might seem at first glance, it proves most telling upon inquiring into the perception of artistic work as being normal—but quite special, after all. The fact that one could even find this astonishing and possibly even a springboard for art theoretical ruminations lies in the distinctive use of ordinary language in the field of art. That use is meant both to communicate belonging and to mark difference. It indicates being part of everyday life as much as being apart from it. The formulation implies a specific understanding of a work of art as well as knowing what goes into producing it. It emphasizes a certain conformity to a social standard and is a positively demonstrative indication that artists work and live just like everybody else. It could, of course, simply be a throwaway phrase. Although its frequency alone is quite enough to contradict that assumption, there is also the fact that artistic output is almost always classified as "work" in contrast to the occasional, earlier use of "(handi)craft." This is an iteration of a certain normalization that is reinforced with every respective reiteration. Hardly anyone realizes that it may once have indicated an agenda, and yet, this was most certainly the case in 1953 when the studios and flats were built at Wuhrstrasse 8/10 in Zurich at the height of postwar modernism in Switzerland.

Considerable political persuasion was required before painters and sculptors could actually begin living and working in their housing cooperative of the 1950s—not least in order to acquire a building site and financial backing. In the following, I take a plea made by the architect Alfred Roth prior to the Wuhrstrasse project[1] as the point of departure in considering how artistic work has been normalized since postwar modernism. Roth was known at the time for his modern design of the Doldertal apartment houses in Zurich as well as publications such as *Die Neue Architektur*.[2] The buildings of the cooperative and the surrounding neighborhood in Zurich-Wiedikon will serve as an occasional point of reference—a built argument as it were—for the current, heated debate on this issue. In his article "Wer soll Künstlerateliers bauen?" (Who should build artists' studios?), Roth unsurprisingly highlights Ernst Gisel's proposal for cooperative flats and studios not far from Zurich (a forerunner, as it were, of the Wuhrstrasse project) as exemplary for the role of artistic work "in today's society."[3] Roth's article does not simply put in a general plea for public support of artistic life and work. Based on the development of working quarters for artists since the 19th century, it is, in fact, about nothing less than a matter of exemplary parallelism between artistic work and forms of modern architecture: modern architecture as the embodiment of a new standard of life and work—without exception. Instead of "stinking backyards" and "amusing rooms" in the center of medieval towns that accommodate "dubious characters," modern artistic work now takes place "in spick-and-span studios" where only the "best and most renowned painters and sculptors work and live."[4] The new domicile for artists is not the expression of bohemian life at a deliberate remove from society but now stands for the rapport, assimilation, and indeed integration of artistic work "into society and its rules."[5] On one hand, Roth was clearly attempting to allay the widespread fears, entertained by the board members of cooperatives and government financiers, of the debauched, uncertain lives of artists and, on the other, to submit unmistakable evidence of a historical break.

---

[1] Alfred Roth, "Wer soll Künstlerateliers bauen?" in *Werk* 35 (1948), vol. 12, pp. 369–374.

[2] Alfred Roth, ed., *Die Neue Architektur. Dargestellt an 20 Beispielen*, Les Editions d'Architecture, Erlenbach/Zurich, 1946.

[3] Ibid., p. 370.
[4] Ibid., pp. 373f.
[5] Ibid., p. 373.

While bohemians of the nineteenth century—and related artistic tendencies of aestheticism—cultivated a maximum of detachment from the industrial work world, the modernist avant-garde in the early twentieth century advocated quite the opposite in certain programs that aimed to integrate artistic work into an industrialized society as efficiently as possible. In positive terms, one might say that industrial principles were enlisted to establish a rapport between forms of work and life but also between art, architecture, and a nascent discipline of design.[6] A new self-understanding of artistic work often went hand-in-hand with new designs for a productive life. It is not surprising that specialists in modernist design repeatedly give a voice to Henry Ford and Frederick W. Taylor, well-known protagonists of industrial rationalization. For instance, Sigfried Giedion, as of the late 1920s, contributed substantially to the spread and international network of modernism in Switzerland. His manifesto *Befreites Wohnen* (Liberated Living) begins with a Ford quotation,[7] while Taylor's theory of rationalizing the organization of work according to scientific principles plays an important role in Giedion's historical survey *Mechanization Takes Command*.[8] Not only is housing to be "liberated" from darkness, crowding, and poor ventilation; people are to be liberated as well—from the useless task of laborious maintenance.[9] At the same time, the distinction between living and working—in Gideon's words, between "productive" and "private" life[10]—is to be eliminated. Personal space—once a place to retreat from professional demands and efforts—would also be optimized as a place of (re-)production. Does that mean that the logic of industrial work in modernism will now invade all areas of life, and work will therefore be carried out everywhere, all the time, and thus in ever-growing quantities? Or does it perhaps herald the optimistic economic vision of a future in which less and less work will have to be done thanks to technological and social progress?[11]

In the 1950s, many protagonists of modern design still saw themselves following the progressive path of industrial rationalization with the intention of establishing a rapport between cultural and other forms of work or even eliminating the separation of life and work altogether. The approach to modern design was often interdisciplinary, to the extent of suggesting a universal concept of design. The ideal of a creatively active and efficiently organized "good" consumer would become reality. But instead of proclaiming a future of modernist liberation, as Giedion did in the 1920s, the mid-twentieth century saw a more moderate, pragmatic belief in the—at least partially—successful normalization of artistic work. This process of normalization applied not only to society's understanding of what artists do but, increasingly, also to the work organization and product marketing of major concerns. While social economics and standards of the 1950s normalized the understanding of artistic work, companies focused increasingly on such artistic principles as self-regulation, creativity, and flexibility. The creative subjects of Western industrial nations did not "find their soul in their automobile, hi-fi set, split-level home, kitchen equipment,"[12] as Herbert Marcuse once summed up the new conditions of postwar modernism, but rather in creative work whose boundaries were increasingly permeable to newly acquired free time.[13] While this may have attenuated the utopian pathos of modernist visions of liberation, it was certainly not merely due to the normalization of the modernist project but perhaps also a consequence of the devastating industrial logic that prevailed in the Second World War. Moreover, Swiss protagonists of modernism in the 1930s and 1940s hardly enjoyed the widespread public support ascribed to them today by current popular marketing. On the contrary, many barely eked out a living not only because there was little demand for their work and correspondingly few commissions but also because they often offended the sensibilities of regional traditionalists and diehard anti-Communists.[14] In contrast to the international modernism championed by Siegfried Giedion, Alfred Roth's writing, as in his support of a publicly funded artists' colony, might be read as a pragmatic compromise with various social tendencies in postwar Zurich.[15]

Cf. Sigfried Giedion, *Befreites Wohnen*, ll Füssli, Zurich, 1929.
Ibid., p. 3.
Sigfried Giedion, *Mechanization Takes nmand, a contribution to anonymous history*, Oxford University Press, New York, 1970, pp. 122ff.
Giedion 1929, p. 5.
Ibid., p. 10.
A vision, already suggested by Karl x, which would be brought about through communist ration from capitalist division of labor and the financial essity to work. See, for example, Karl Marx, Friedrich els, "Die Deutsche Ideologie," in *Karl Marx. Friedrich els. Werke,* vol. 3, Dietz Verlag, Berlin, 1978, p. 33. In the first half of the twentieth century, less radical economists like John Maynard Keynes expressed the conviction that there would be increasingly less necessary work for future generations. John Maynard Keynes, "Economic possibilities for our grandchildren," in *Revisiting Keynes*, eds. Lorenzo Pecchi, Gustavo Piga, MIT Press, Cambridge MA/London, 2008, pp. 17–26.
12 Herbert Marcuse, *One-Dimensional Man. Studies in the Ideology of Advanced Industrial Society*, chapter 1, Beacon, Boston, 1964. https://www.marcuse.org/herbert/pubs/64onedim/odm1.html (accessed April 24, 2021)
13 Andreas Reckwitz, "The psychological turn in creativity: From the pathological genius to the normalisation of the self as resource," in *The Invention of Creativity. Modern Society and the Culture of the New*, Polity, Cambridge, 2017, chapter 5.
14 One of the most biting attacks came at the time from Alexander von Senger, architect of the Swiss-Re building in Zurich, 1914, and fervent Nazi during the Second World War, who discredited the Neues Bauen movement as "a torch from Moscow." Alexander von Senger, *Die Brandfackel Moskaus*, Kaufhaus, Zurzach, 1931.
15 I am indebted to Stanislaus von Moos's evaluation in his introduction to *Alfred Roth. Architekt der Kontinuität*, Waser Verlag, Zurich 1985, pp. 9–34, pp. 20f.

Friedrich Kuhn in his studio a few months before his death, photographed by H.R. Giger, 1972

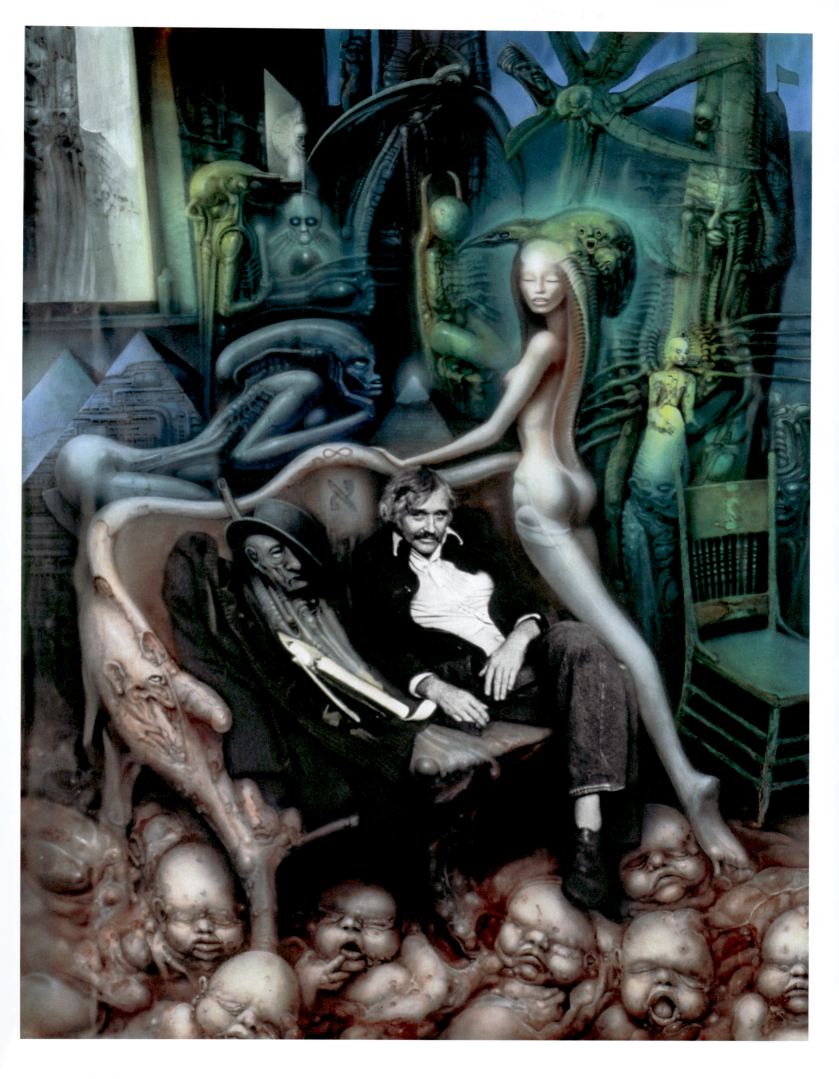

H.R. Giger, *Friedrich Kuhn II, 1973*, acrylic on paper on wood, 1973

1   Otto Morach at his preview, Galerie Henri Wengér, 1970   2   Tildy Grob-Wengér, preview, Galerie Henri Wengér, c. 1967   3   Otto Teucher in his studio, 1977/78   4   In Otto Teucher's studio, 1977/78

1   Painter, graphic artist, and draftsman Werner W. Wyss in his studio, 1977/78

2   Friedrich Kuhn at the stairs to the second-floor studios with his sculpture *Palme* for the legendary exhibition *Die Palmen des Friedrich Kuhn*, 1969

3   In Friedrich Kuhn's studio, c. 1969

Thus, in the 1950s, efforts can be observed to socially integrate—i.e., normalize—artistic work, whereby the boundaries between different social sectors seem particularly permeable, as between industry and art, mass production and individual creativity, and work and free time. On the other hand, it also becomes apparent that the utopian aspirations of the 1920s to overcome all material and social constraints through the principles of industrialized work were not achieved. Instead, the contradictions became all the more apparent. This is revealed, not least, in the understanding of artistic work: care was taken to remain set apart, even though modernist programs rigorously sought to conform to industrial structures—and in Switzerland, to those of a capitalist social state. Even in his impassioned plea for new forms of artistic work, Alfred Roth describes the studio as a "sacred place" for "the noblest and most sublime endeavors a creative person can produce."[16] In fact, he even writes about the "primacy of the fine arts in cultural life and of the artist in today's society."[17] In addition to the modern narrative of artistic work productively integrated into the operations of well-organized daily life, the architect also insists on its transcendental, quasi-religious character and its divine place in society. And when Roth applies conventional art historical genres to the "painters and sculptors" of his time, he not only couches his argument in anachronistic terminology but also—in view of the increasingly blurred boundaries between genres and materials—avails himself of a long-outdated concept of "work." The latter had already become obsolete by the beginning of the twentieth century thanks to the avant-garde and, moreover, contradicts Roth's remarks on the fundamentally changed character of artistic work. Apparently, the idealism of the nineteenth century, which lent greater value to creative activity (especially art and philosophy) than to any other work and, in fact, declared it the very goal of human existence, has not only outlived all modern tendencies toward normalization, but has actually become still more radical.[18] Doesn't this patently contradict a program of normalization in which artists live and work like everyone else?

The shape of the Wuhrstrasse buildings is also subject to ambiguous interpretation. The sawtooth roof of the studios suggests the typology of a factory while the secluded, backyard location, walled off and with an inwardly oriented ground plan, seems to be inspired by monastery architecture. The simplicity of the ground plans, construction, and materials could be read as a response to the dictates of efficiency in industrial production as well as a quasi-religious exercise in modesty and renunciation. The immediate environs are, however, dominated by the major architectural modifications that occurred in the wake of industrialization towards the end of the nineteenth and in the early twentieth centuries, transforming the once rural community of Wiedikon into a burgeoning urban neighborhood. Small tradesmen can still be found today in some of the inner courtyards and, until just a few decades ago, several larger factories were still in operation on the margins of this neighborhood.

One could object that Alfred Roth's inquiry into who should build artists' studios represents a merely subjective defense of certain preferences regarding artistic life and work in the mid-twentieth century. Especially well-meaning journalistic support for former staff member and later architect of the Wuhrstrasse complex, Ernst Gisel, may also have played a role. Roth certainly lays no claim to a universally valid theory of modern artistic work and its housing. Nonetheless, his prominence and substantial influence as a journalist does give me cause to speculate that a programmatic quality underlies his plea; additionally, his argument shares common ground with similar, mid-twentieth century reflections on artistic work. In the 1950s, Max Bill defended both the individual genius of artistic work as well as its integration into the modern standards of the principles of industrial production.[19] In this respect, Roth's remarks on work could be read as symptomatic of broader social developments, which increasingly idealized the active—and in modern terms, working—person in general.

---

16 Alfred Roth, 1946 (see note 2 above), p. 374.

17 Ibid.

18 I am referring particularly to G.W. F. Hegel's idealization of spiritual, creative activity, which has been variously criticized (e.g., by Karl Marx), but nonetheless continues to make an appearance in our philosophical writings (as in Conceptual Art).

19 Cf. Max Bill, *FORM. A Balance Sheet of Mid-Twentieth Century Trends in Design*, Karl Werner, Basel, 1952.

In the 1950s, Hannah Arendt introduced the concept of *vita activa* to describe the modern approach to life, which foregrounds work instead of contemplation and leisure, as the "the most esteemed of all human activities."[20] According to Arendt, this esteem is, in fact, so great that gainful employment is the only modern activity to be taken seriously,[21] which means, conversely, that "every activity unconnected with labor becomes a hobby."[22] Although Arendt explicitly mentions that artistic "workers" are the only acceptable exception,[23] one can well imagine how great the social pressure of normalization must have been on artists as well. What's more, this tendency met not only with resistance, some artists actually embraced it. Since the beginning of the twentieth century, principles of industrial work and production were repeatedly proclaimed as the agenda and goal of artistic artwork—specifically in the form of Constructivism and Concrete Art. Regardless of whether artists embraced or opposed this approach, the "industrial condition" would become a self-evident, determining factor in the twentieth century not only as applied to individual works but to contemporary art in general.[24] Similarly, when the Baugenossenschaft Maler und Bildhauer Zürich (the Painters and Sculptors Building Cooperative Zurich) was founded, the studios and apartments at Wuhrstrasse became a location shared by a wide variety of artistic approaches—some incorporating materials and techniques that showed a close relationship to industrial principles of production, and others less so. Indeed, the deliberate emphasis, in some cases, on traditional artistic qualities—in terms of handicraft or embeddedness in traditional genres such as painting and sculpture—could even be seen as unabashed opposition to any adaptation to the circumstances of modern industrial production. But in the mid-1950s they all moved into the same modern architectural complex. Recalling Alfred Roth's plea for the implementation of a cooperative project a few years earlier, different forms of art had actually come together under the heading of the cultural and political argument of normalization—despite certain contradictions.

The wide-ranging normalization of work in the wake of modernism is clearly connected with the establishment of new social norms, but it is certainly not a one-way street heading in the direction of industrial efficiency. The nearly transcendental idealization of creative output, found in Roth's plea for a colony of "painters and sculptors" in Zurich, is indicative of significant movement from the opposite direction—from the social context assigned to artist bohemians in the nineteenth century. It is a sphere of artistic autonomy and creativity in which artists live (and are meant to live) in opposition to bourgeois values, where the "rules of art"[25] regarding work and added value are reversed. The success of life and work is not measured by financial gain but by an almost demonstrative monetary disinterest. The greatest gain is promised by a precarious, but deliberately nonconformist life under the aegis of personal eccentricity and ingenious creativity—albeit in a different currency, namely that of "symbolic capital."[26] This is, of course, an abridged juxtaposition to the bourgeois working world. For Pierre Bourdieu, who bases his argument on a retrospective look at the nineteenth century, specifically explores the relations between the field of art and the industrially defined, capitalist economic system. My somewhat pointed representation of the two poles is intended, on one hand, as a reminder of the reversal of economic values in the cultural field—a point of departure for setting oneself apart in ongoing opposition. On the other hand, this demarcation in the field of art proves to be a resource for developments in other social fields as well. For decades, cultural critics denounced the logic of capitalism for encroaching on the supposedly autonomous zone of cultural work.[27] That same argument reappeared in the late 1990s in controversies about work in postindustrial capitalism—but now in reverse. Artistic life and work were seen as a role model, with independent creativity, flexibility, and networking increasingly regarded as standard qualifications.

Hannah Arendt, *The Human Condition*, versity of Chicago Press, Chicago, 1998, p. 101.
Ibid., p. 127.
Ibid, p. 128.
Ibid.
Burkhard Meltzer, *Das ausgestellte ›en. Design in Kunstdiskursen nach den Avantgarden, ›mos, Berlin, 2020.*

25 Pierre Bourdieu, *The Rules of Art: Genesis and Structure of the Literary Field*, Stanford University Press, 1996.
26 Ibid.

27 I am thinking particularly of the inestimable influence of Theodor W. Adorno and Max Horkheimer, whose writings on the culture industry were seminal to the reception and, above all, the criticism of these conditions in the second half of the twentieth century. Max Horkheimer, Theodor W. Adorno, "The Culture Industry: Enlightenment as Mass Deception," in *Dialectic of Enlightenment*, Stanford University Press, 2002.

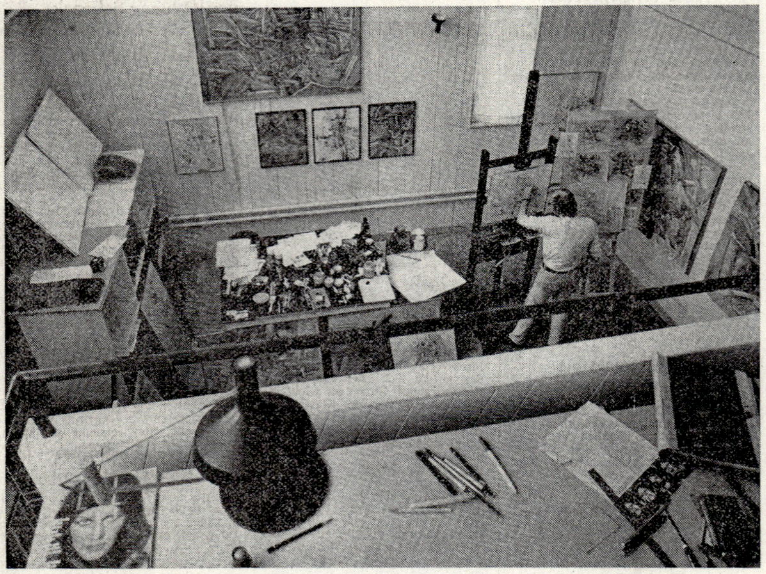

Im Atelier von Werner W. Wyss. Die Malerateliers weisen eine über eine Treppe erreichbare Zeichnungsnische auf.

Von der Jeremiade zum Musterbau

Die Künstlergenossenschaft an der Wuhrstrasse / Von Peter Killer

Die Häuser Wuhrstrasse 8 und 10 werden von Architekten, Künstlern und Kulturreferenten aus aller Welt besucht. In Zürich selbst sind die Bauten und deren Nutzung fast nur den Bewohnern und Anwohnern bekannt. Eine Ausstellung im Foyer des Kunsthauses Zürich macht auf die vor 25 Jahren realisierte Utopie einer Künstlergenossenschaft aufmerksam. Peter Killer hat sich mit den Initianten der Baugenossenschaft Maler und Bildhauer Zürich und Bewohnern der Häuser unterhalten und versucht, die Motive und die Geschichte dieser Unternehmung nachzuzeichnen.

Die drei mussten sich wie Hochstapler vorkommen. Zwei von ihnen hatten selten mehr als fünfzig Rappen im Sack, der dritte brachte es – so meint er heute – im Durchschnitt auf 55 Rappen. Und doch waren sind ständig unterwegs, um Bauplätze zu begutachten, standen mit Architekten im Gespräch, hatten Zusammenkünfte mit den Behörden, kurz: sie unternahmen alles, was zu den Vorbereitungen gehört, wenn man bauen will. Die drei Künstler *Otto Teucher, Otto Müller* und *Max Truninger* entwickelten sich zu versierten Kennern der Bauprobleme.

Was war es, das die beiden Bildhauer und den Maler in Bauwut versetzt hatte? Ihnen war die Erfahrung gemeinsam, wie schwierig es ist, in Zürich ein Atelier zu finden. In den dreissiger Jahren hatte es in Zürich noch das «Venedigli» gegeben. Eine grossartige Sache, meinen die drei Künstler übereinstimmend. Da hatte ein ehemaliger Maurer, der nun tagaus, tagein im sauberen Ueberkleid am Flügel sass und sang, von den SBB den ehemaligen Bahnhof Enge gemietet und den Künstlern weitervermietet. Germaine Richier, Varlin und andere Prominente und weniger Prominente arbeiteten dort und genossen die Atmosphäre, die durch die enge Künstlernachbarschaft entstanden war. In Otto Teucher, Otto Müller und Max Truninger blieb die Erinnerung an dieses leider nicht lange existierende, bald abgerissene Künstlerhaus wach.

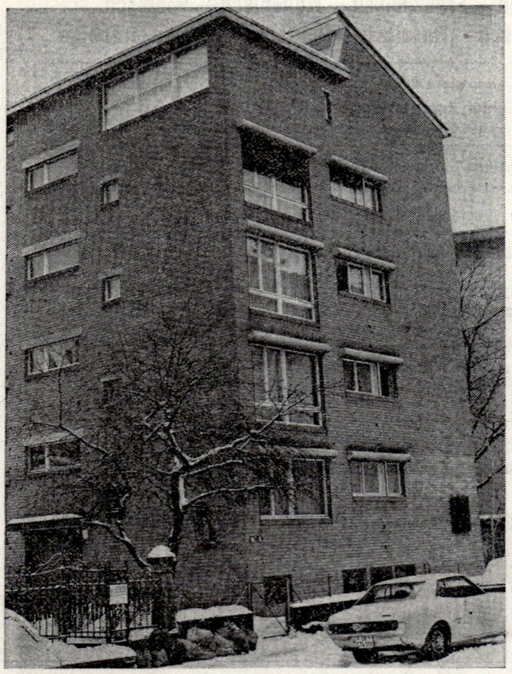

1952 hat Ernst Gisel für die Baugenossenschaft Maler und Bildhauer Zürich an der Wuhrstrasse 8 und 10 ein Wohn- und Atelierhaus gebaut. 12 Ateliers und 8 Wohnungen stehen hier Künstlern zur Verfügung. (Bilder Schlatter)

Die Künstler wechselten von einem Atelier ins andere. Sie kamen sich vor, als wären sie der Ewige Jude persönlich, nur dass sie im Gegensatz zu diesem noch von Ballast, nämlich unverkauften und angefangenen Werken, begleitet waren. Otto Müller blieb sogar einmal während acht Monaten ohne Atelier. Eine grauenhafte Zeit, erinnert er sich. Atelierlos war er geworden, weil er, ohne den Hausbesitzer zu fragen, den Werkplatz vergrössert hatte, zusammen mit seinem Gesellen Paul Grass ein Stückchen Garten mit der grossen Walze eingeebnet hatte.

Doch war es nicht allein das Unstete, das die Künstler störte. Der Mangel an geeigneten Arbeitsräumen zwang sie, dort ein Atelier zu mieten, wo sich immer der Glücksfall anbot. Ganz egal, ob einem Quartier und Nachbarschaft gefielen oder nicht. Inmitten von Bürgerhäusern seien sie sich dann wie Menschen aus einer andern Welt vorgekommen, hätten sie das Gefühl gehabt, sich ständig der eigenen Haut wehren zu müssen.

Selbsthilfeaktion ohne Vorbild

Es blieb nicht beim Lamento. Aus den Jeremiaden wurde schliesslich der Plan, eine Baugenossenschaft zu gründen. Völlig mittellos liessen sich 1949 Teucher, Müller und Truninger ins Handelsregister eintragen. Von nun an gab es eine Baugenossenschaft Maler und Bildhauer Zürich. Die eine Voraussetzung für das Gelingen des Projekts war gegeben. Die drei Initianten kannten einen jungen, begabten Architekten: *Ernst Gisel*. Er hatte sich bereit erklärt, mit Rat und Tat behilflich zu sein. Wesentlich schwieriger war es, ohne Geld Bauland zu finden. Auch das billigste Terrain wäre ihnen zu teuer gewesen. Und hinzu kam, dass sich die drei Künstler geschworen hatten, sich nicht aus der Stadt verdrängen zu lassen, möglichst nah beim Zentrum zu bleiben.

Sie sprachen bei der Stadt Zürich vor. Der Name Baugenossenschaft Maler und Bildhauer Zürich machte einen zwiespältigen Eindruck. Gegen den vorderen Teil des Namens sprach nichts: damals war ja die hohe Zeit der genossenschaftlichen Bauaktivitäten. Und Stadtrat Peter, dem die Finanzabteilung unterstellt war, galt als überzeugter Förderer der Baugenossenschaften. Der hintere Teil des Namens weckte allerdings weniger Vertrauen. Mit einem Atelierhaus am Hirschengraben, auf dem Areal des heutigen Swissair-Gebäudes, waren nicht durchwegs positive Erfahrungen gemacht worden. Das von den Künstlern selbst verwaltete Haus schien den Behörden kein Musterbeispiel zu sein, das ähnliche Experimente rechtfertigte.

Schliesslich kam es doch zum Vertrag. Otto Müller fasst die Ereignisse wie folgt zusammen:

«Im Frühjahr 1952 hat der Stadtrat von Zürich mit der Genossenschaft einen Vertrag über die Abtretung eines Stückes Bauland von 1285,8 qm an der Wuhrstrasse im Baurecht auf die Dauer von 80 Jahren gegen einen Baurechtszins von 3½% und über den Bau eines Atelier- und Wohnhauses mit 12 Ateliers und 8 Wohnungen nach Plänen von Architekt Ernst Gisel abgeschlossen.

Das Vorhaben konnte nur unter namhafter finanzieller Hilfe des Kantons und der Stadt Zürich durchgeführt werden. Die gesamte Bausumme betrug 463 000 Fr., wovon die Stadt die erste und die zweite Hypothek übernahm. Die Genossenschaft selbst konnte immerhin ein symbolisches Kapital von 28 000 Fr. aufbringen. Dies wurde ermöglicht durch die Werbung von Genossenschaftern, die einen Beitrag von 100 Fr. zu entrichten hatten, und durch Zeichnung von Anteilscheinen der Mieter in der ungefähren Höhe eines Jahreszinses des gemieteten Objekts. Mit dem Bau des Hauses wurde Mitte Juli 1952 begonnen, und im März 1953 konnten die Ateliers bezogen werden.»

Die Mieter der ersten Stunde waren *Otto Morach, Oskar Dalvit, Otto Müller, Trudi Demut, Carlotta Stocker, Hans Rohner, Carlo Vivarelli, Otto Teucher, Tildy Grob* und *Bruno Heller.*

Ausser diesen Genossenschaftsbauten gab es kaum neue Häuser im überalterten Quartier. Den Künstlern gefiel das Quartier nicht, dem Quartier gefielen die Künstler nicht. Eine Baueinsprache eines Lehrers aus der Nachbarschaft blockierte den Fortgang der Angelegenheit, und als das Haus fertig war, gab das oft etwas laute Treiben einigen Nachbarn immer wieder Anlass, die Polizei an die Wuhrstrasse zu rufen.

Stürmische Anfänge

An der Wuhrstrasse ist ein Stück Zürcher Kunstgeschichte geschrieben worden. Otto Morach arbeitete hier in aller Stille. Manchmal mischte er sich bei Festen unter die Künstlernachbarn. Trudi Demut: «Ich habe etwa fünfmal an Atelierfesten mit ihm Duzis gemacht, anderntags traute ich mich dann aber doch nicht, ihn mit ‚Sali' zu grüssen, und nannte ihn wieder ‚Herr Morach'.» Und Otto Teucher erinnert sich, dass kaum ein Kollege ins Atelier treten durfte. Wenn er als Hauswart von Morach gerufen wurde, seien jeweils alle Bilder zur Wand gedreht gewesen. Als der Augenarzt dem Maler verordnete, er müsse viel ins Grüne schauen, zog er mit Schnüren die Aeste eines am Fenster vorbeiwachsenden Baumes in sein Blickfeld. Dieser Anblick habe vermuten lassen, Armand Schulthess sei aus dem Tessin an die Wuhrstrasse übersiedelt.

Silvio Mattioli, der im 1. Stock ein Maleratelier gemietet hatte, schmiedete zur Freude der Künstler und zum Aerger der Nachbarschaft auf dem Werkplatz von Otto Teucher. Je mehr das Œuvre wuchs, desto grösser wurde die Stätte des Wirkens. Sie dehnte sich am Atelier von Morach und Dalvit vorbei aus und kam erst dort zum Halt, wo Otto Müller der Expansion mit der eigenen Arbeit einen Riegel schob. Die Situation eskalierte dann, als plötzlich vor dem Atelier des feinsinnigen Dalvit ein Kran stand, den Mattioli herbeigeschafft hatte.

Silvio Mattioli war es auch, der Otto Müller half, die Granit-Kuh für das Friesenberg-Schulhaus fertigzustellen. Da die Arbeit zu keinem Ende gekommen war, liess die Stadt Zürich das Werk unvollendet aufstellen. So brachen nun Otto Müller und Silvio Mattioli tagtäglich ins Friesenberg-Quartier auf, nach Alaska, wie sie sagten, denn die Atmosphäre war entsprechend eisig. Diese Situation brachte es mit sich, dass die Aufenthalte in der Wirtschaft in die Länge gezogen wurden.

Anfang der sechziger Jahre kam *Friedrich Kuhn* an die Wuhrstrasse. Mit Bewunderung und Achtung sprechen die Wuhrsträssler von ihrem toten Hausgenossen. Hier entstand ein guter Teil von Friedrich Kuhns Hauptwerk. Kuhn war eine Kristallisationsfigur der Geselligkeit. Otto Müller und Trudi Demut erinnern sich an einen aussergewöhnlichen Abend im Demut-Atelier. Eine ganze Reihe von angefangenen Figuren stand im Raum. Fritz Kuhn und Silvio Mattioli kamen mit einem Velo durch die Türe. Fritz setzte sich aufs Velo, Silvio setzte sich auf Fritz. Sie begannen zwischen den fragilen Skulpturen Schlaufen und Kurven zu fahren, liessen nicht mehr ab davon, und all dies sei so sachte und behutsam geschehen, dass man nicht einen Augenblick daran gedacht habe, es könnte irgend etwas Schaden nehmen. Schliesslich habe man zu viert das Fahrrad mit Gips und Bändern verziert. Ein schöneres Velo könne man sich nicht denken. Anderer Ansicht war der Besitzer. Auf Rechnung der Künstler verwandelte der Velomechaniker das potentielle Museumsstück in ein fahrtüchtiges Vehikel zurück.

Die Ateliers an der Wuhrstrasse liegen wie Klosterzellen nebeneinander. Klösterlich ist auch die Stille, die heute hier herrscht. Die architektonische Organisation hat das harmonische Zusammenleben erleichtert. Heute würde man möglicherweise dazu neigen, die Architektur offener zu gestalten, für die gemeinsamen Interessen auch gemeinsame Räume bereitzustellen. Dass dies vor 25 Jahren nicht geschehen ist, lässt sich einerseits aus den zwischenmenschlichen Vorbedingungen verstehen. Die Atelierisolation bildete den Ausgleich zum kontaktintensiven Alltag. Vor allem aber waren die Wuhrsträssler mindestens 15 Jahre lang – Otto Morach ausgenommen – so knapp bei Kasse, dass jeglicher Raumluxus ausser Betracht lag. Die Situation, dass heute renommierte Künstler ihre Miete mit dem besten Willen erst nach monatelanger Verzögerung zahlen konnten, war nicht unvertraut.

Gemeinschaftlichkeit ergab sich von selbst. Als Friedrich Kuhn seine beiden grossen Expo-Bilder nicht fertigbekam, malten Mattioli, Trudi Demut und Otto Müller unter Kuhns Regie in der Nacht vor dem Transport nach Lausanne das Werk gemeinsam zu Ende.

Die Wuhrstrasse-Baukolonie wurde gegründet, um Malern und Bildhauern materiell vorteilhafte und harmonische Arbeits- und Wohnmöglichkeiten zu sichern. Die Ateliers sind noch heute preiswert. Dass der Geist der Siedlung nach wie vor eine fruchtbare Arbeit erlaubt, demonstriert die Ausstellung, die bis zum 29. März im Kunsthaus zu sehen ist.

BRENNPUNKT

Wegbereiter ohne Nachfolger?

Die Idee der Künstlerbaugenossenschaft fasziniert auch heute noch. Und trotzdem ist diese Idee einsam geblieben. Selbst wenn die Atelierprobleme heute in Zürich grösser sind denn je.

Seit 1952 gibt es die Baugenossenschaft Maler und Bildhauer Zürich. Als die Initianten nach einigen Jahren erkannten, dass die Idee tragfähig war, fassten sie den Entschluss, weiterzubauen, noch mehr Ateliers und Wohnungen bereitzustellen. Ernst Gisel arbeitete ein weiteres Projekt aus. Rasch zeigte sich aber, dass auch bei bescheidensten Bedürfnissen die Erstellungskosten so hoch waren, dass nur noch privilegierte Künstler, die ohnehin ein Atelier finden, die Miete hätten bezahlen können. So wurden dann diese Baupläne beerdigt.

Unterdessen hat sich die Konjunktursituation wieder verändert. Die realisierte Wuhrstrasseutopie müsste eigentlich den Mut geben, noch einmal recht tüchtig zu träumen, müsste junge Künstler anregen, neue Lösungen für die jetzigen Atelierprobleme zu suchen. In Basel wurde in jüngerer Zeit mit der Umwandlung der alten Kaserne Klingenthal in ein Atelierhaus Wegweisendes geleistet. Die ehemaligen Kantonnemente dienen nun als Arbeitsräume. Für 100 Franken im Monat können die Künstler über einen 70 qm grossen Arbeitsraum und über zusätzliche Lagerfläche verfügen.

Die Bereitstellung von Ateliers ist eine der effektivsten Formen der Kulturförderung. Während Stipendien und Ankäufe nur punktuell wirken und immer leistungsbezogen sind, ist die Ateliervermietung zu günstigen Bedingungen eine über lange Zeit hin nützliche Hilfe, die auch dann nicht aussetzt, wenn es vorbei ist mit Stipendien (bei bestimmten Alterslimiten) oder mit Ankäufen (etwa bei einer Schaffenskrise).

An der Wuhrstrasse und bei der Basler Klingenthal-Kaserne ging die Initiative von den Künstlern aus. Zürichs junge Künstler müssten sich von den beiden gelungenen Experimenten provoziert fühlen.

Peter Killer

Tages-Anzeiger, Saturday, March 4, 1978

Painter and draftsman René Ed. Brauchli with Trudi Demut in the courtyard of the cooperative, 1974

René Ed. Brauchli and painter and draftsman Remo Roth in the courtyard of the cooperative, 1974

1   The sculpture *Phänotyp II* in Otto Müller's studio, 1982

2   Otto Müller in his studio; behind him *Mädchenkopf* and *Phänotyp II*, c. 1982

3   Painter and art teacher Hansjörg Mattmüller in the door of his studio, 1977/78

1   In Trudi Demut's studio, 1988

2   Trudi Demut, 1986

3   In Trudi Demut's studio with sculptures *Tisch II* and *Konvexer Tisch III* (unfinished), 1988

4   Painter Bert Schmidmeister in his studio, 1975/76

New forms of work that characterize an increasingly digitally networked, postindustrial service society now take their cue from much that was still considered as contrary to the working world in the nineteenth century—with one exception: the financially disinterested bohemian. This anti-figure is as unlikely to have survived in the everyday working life of most freelance artists as it has in the human resources departments of major corporations. Apart from this one exception, many principles that were once the exclusive preserve of art have become the new normal. The unprecedented expansion and pronounced political function of so-called creative industries since the 1990s illustrate the exemplary role of artistic work; just think of the role played by design, art, and media in global location marketing.[28] Artists often contribute to projects initiated, for example, by newly opened museums or biennials. Whether in frequently changing, project-related engagements or as the vanguard of urban real-estate development in former industrial neighborhoods, artists not only embody a new norm in determining their own creative and flexible working conditions; they are also strategically exploited as an enhancement, as a factor that adds value to the location. This applies particularly to the Wiedikon district of Zurich. A new feeder road has calmed traffic and two large industrial plants have been repurposed over the past twenty years, upgrading the neighborhood and ensuring a steady rise in real estate prices. In the immediate vicinity of Wuhrstrasse, condominiums, a spa, a shopping mall, and Google's European headquarters now occupy land that once accommodated a large brewery and a paper factory.

Today, however, only few artists can reap enough benefit from their contribution to the upgrading process to keep their neighborhood studios and flats in the long term. And current buzzwords that characterize artistic work, such as post-studio or even post-internet, suggest these flexible creative workers no longer even need this form of real-estate stability since they are always ahead of the game as the avant-garde of prevailing work forms. There are no doubt positive aspects of this flexibility, for instance, as a welcome opportunity for individual emancipation from the uniform optimization programs of industrial modernity[29] or even as an attempt to implant forms of critical, artistic action into the social and economic field.[30] This flexibility could also be criticized as clever exploitation of art and artists by a social state dismantled through neoliberalism or by real-estate companies—more or less as effective PR replacement for slashed social funding.[31] Others voice concern that artistic work, as an all-encompassing role model, is rather more like an aesthetic assault on the social field that could lead to all-embracing social aestheticization.[32]

The two fields actually do interrelate in many respects: living is like working in that it is not by nature random but subject to certain forms. And art is produced under specific social circumstances. Artistic work no doubt often entails precarious living conditions—even if many artists commit to this situation by choice and enjoy the freedom related to it.[33] Working conditions elsewhere are different, particularly in the low-wage sector or digitally organized sharing economy where precarious circumstances are aggravated by the long-term social consequences of the model of artistic creativity and flexibility. One can naturally choose to accept or reject a job in this case as well, but the personal background that leads to the decision makes a significant difference. Isabell Lorey observes another difference from the precarity of the latter working conditions in the twofold motivation for so-called "precarity by choice": the combination of the freedom of self-fulfillment and the diffuse feeling of contributing to a higher, indeed transcendental "good" called culture.[34] Flashes of the idealistic transfiguration of artistic work still appear in the contemporary processes of normalization that I have here described. It is therefore impossible to judge how dramatic the future change will be in the relationship between idealization and normalization—in fact normality in general, regarding work, added value, flexibility, and mobility.

---

[28] Andreas Reckwitz, "Creative Cities: Culturalising Urban Life," in Reckwitz 2017, pp. 173–200.
[29] Thus Antonio Negri/Michael Hardt no longer speak of the human masses of modernity but rather of the "multitude" of the present—a largely self-governing entity, where individual forms of expression are exchanged via networks, while simultaneously ensuring that one belongs to the "multitude." Antonio Negri/Michael Hardt, "Multitude," in *Multitude: War and Democracy in the Age of the Empire*, Penguin Press, New York, 2004, pp. 97–228.
[30] Cf. the much cited analysis of the relationship between art criticism and social criticism in Luc Boltanski/Ève Chiapello, *The New Spirit of Capitalism*, Verso, 2018.
[31] Claire Bishop, *Artificial Hells*, Verso, London/New York, 2012, pp. 14f.
[32] Reckwitz, 2012.
[33] Isabell Lorey, "Vom immanenten Widerspruch zur hegemonialen Funktion. Biopolitische Gouvernementalität und Selbst-Prekarisierung von KulturproduzentInnen," in *Kritik der Kreativität*, eds. Ulf Wuggenig, Gerald Raunig, transversal texts, piano, 2016, pp. 257–282, p. 261.
[34] Ibid., p. 260.

Otto Müller at work on *Grosser Kopf* for the Fellbach town hall/D, c. 1985

Der Künstler und sein (noch nicht fertiges) Werk: Bildhauer Otti Müller und Frauenskulptur.

Die Malerin Tildy Wenger begeistert sich noch heute für die schönen Räume.

Schätzt die angenehme Atmosphäre: der Maler Peter Stiefel.

Der Maler René Brauchli zählt zu den Neocomern und amtiert als Genossenschaftspräsident.

Leben und leben lassen in der Künstler-Kommune

Die Künstlergenossenschaft an der Wuhrstrasse funktioniert nach dem Igelprinzip, und das seit 35 Jahren

Das aus der Soziologie bekannte Igel-Prinzip besagt, dass Igel in der Kälte zusammenrücken, um wärmer zu haben, dass sie aber nicht allzu nahe zusammenrücken dürfen, weil sie sich sonst stechen würden. Und genau nach diesem Prinzip funktionieren die beiden Atelierhäuser an der Wuhrstrasse nun schon seit 35 Jahren. Zwölf Künstler und Künstlerinnen leben unter einem Dach, junge und alte, bekannte und etwas weniger bekannte, respektieren sich – und halten Distanz.

Am Anfang standen lange und sehr zähe Verhandlungen», erinnert sich der Bildhauer und Kunstpreisträger der Stadt Zürich, *Otto Müller*. «Wir hatten keine Wohnungen, keine Ateliers, kein Geld. Deshalb gründeten wir eine Genossenschaft, die von der Stadt Zürich ein Grundstück im Baurecht erhielt, ferner eine erste und eine zweite Hypothek. Die restlichen finanziellen Mittel kratzten wir selber zusammen.»

Viel Glück hatten die Künstler bei der Wahl des Architekten *Ernst Gisel*, denn dieser schuf im sachlichen Bauhausstil helle, schön-proportionierte Räume, für die sich die Bewohner noch heute begeistern. «Jeder hat sich anders eingerichtet – und alles ist möglich», sagt die Malerin *Tildy Wenger*, die ebenfalls zur ersten Generation der Wuhrstrassen-Künstler gehört. Sie selber hat sich mit einer Überfülle von Büchern, Nippsachen und Kunstgegenständen umgeben, die sie zum Teil geschenkt erhielt, zum Teil von ihren Reisen mitgebracht hat. So gehören zu ihren letzten Errungenschaften ein Fächer, eine Tonfigur und eine Volkstracht aus China. An der Wand aber hängt ein kraftvolles, lebensprühendes Stilleben von der kürzlich verstorbenen *Carlotta Stocker*, die auch im Atelierhaus wohnte. «Sie hatte keine Wohnung, nur das Atelier. Deshalb kochte sie oft bei mir – übrigens ganz ausgezeichnet», erzählt Tildy von ihrer Malerfreundin.

In der brav-bürgerlichen Umgebung nahe beim Manesseplatz fallen die beiden Atelierhäuser kaum auf: ein sauber gekehrter Plattenweg, einige Rosensträucher und blanke Fensterscheiben, also absolut nichts Chaotisch-Künstlerisches. Trotzdem blieben die Proteste der Anwohner nicht aus. «Immer, wenn wir in den fünfziger Jahren ein Fest feierten, schickte man uns die Polizei auf den Hals, erinnern sich die Pioniere. Das allerdings hat sich inzwischen gründlich geändert. Die Nachbarn merkten, dass auch Maler und Bildhauer recht ordentliche Menschen sind. Zudem hörte man immer wieder Ruhmreiches von der Wuhrstrasse: *Hans Aeschbacher* und *Otto Müller* erhielten den Kunstpreis der Stadt Zürich, doch auch *Silvio Matioli, Oskar Dalvit, Trudi Demut, Otto Teucher, Werner W. Wyss, Tildy Wenger* und andere machten sich einen Namen. Das Quartier darf stolz sein.

Bleibt die Frage, warum die Arrivierten nicht in grössere und noblere Behausungen umziehen. Eine Zwei- oder Dreizimmerwohnung plus Atelier oder gar nur ein Atelier mit Schlafplatz und selbstgebastelter Dusche bietet schliesslich – zumindest für Ehepaare mit Kindern – nicht viel Komfort. Doch die Künstler schätzen die angenehme Atmosphäre sowie die extrem niederen Mieten. 70 bis 90 Franken pro Monat wurden in den Anfangsjahren bezahlt, heute sind es etwas mehr als 300 Franken, was wohl noch immer einen Billigkeits-Rekord darstellen dürfte. Kein Wunder, dass für die Ateliers lange Wartelisten existieren, weshalb die Genossenschaft wählerisch sein kann. Sonntagsmaler haben keine Chancen. Wer an der Wuhrstrasse einziehen will, muss sich über eine seriöse künstlerische Karriere ausweisen können.

René Brauchli, Remo Roth und *Peter Stiefel* zählen zu den Newcomern, haben sich jedoch problemlos eingelebt. Brauchli amtet sogar als allgemein anerkannter und beliebter Genossenschaftspräsident.

Versöhnung der Kunstrichtungen

«Wir halten Distanz», sagt Remo Roth. «Jeder pflegt seinen eigenen Stil, jeder lebt für sich, und wenn wir einmal gemeinsam ausstellen, ist das purer Zufall.» Er selber malt Bilder, die er selber als «neo-informell» bezeichnet und die um den Begriff «Schwarz» kreisen. Da werden auf grossformatige Baumwolltücher dunkle Impressionen hingeworfen, aus denen sparsamstes Rot, Grün oder Gelb leuchtet. Doch das Schwarz der Bilder ist nicht bedrohlich, eher meditativ-beruhigend wie das Dunkel der Nacht.

Wenige Meter von Roth entfernt arbeitet Otti Müller an einer Skulptur für die Cafeteria des Universitätsspitals, eine schlanke Frauengestalt mit beschwörerisch ausgebreiteten Armen, die in Messing gegossen werden soll. Man denkt an eine moderne Schutzmantelmadonna, nur eben an eine Schutzmantelmadonna ohne alles mythologische Beiwerk. Ihr Modell steht momentan im sogenannten Bildhauerhof, wo Erdbeeren wachsen und wo Trudi Demut energisch für Ruhe sorgt.

Tildy Wenger wiederum beschäftigt sich in ihrem Dachatelier mit lichtvollen, oft dreidimensionalen Impressionen. Ausgangspunkt sind für sie zumeist Naturphänomene, die sie jedoch völlig verfremdet. So verwandelt sie die Wüste in orange-gelbe Gleichklänge, als wolle sie nicht das äussere, sondern das innere Bild der Sahara gestalten. Drei Künstler, drei Temperamente – und jeder toleriert jeden.

Wie schon eingangs erwähnt: die Künstler-Genossenschaft an der Wuhrstrasse funktioniert nach dem Igelprinzip. Enge Freundschaften wie die von Tildy Wenger und Carlotta Stocker oder von Otti Müller und Trudi Demut kommen zwar vor, sind aber nicht die Regel. Normaler ist der vernünftige Konsens, wie es Otto Müller formuliert hat: «Hinter einer Genossenschaft muss der Wille zur Erreichung eines bestimmten Zieles stehen. In unserem Fall: das Wohnen und Arbeiten der Genossenschafter unter möglichst günstigen ökonomischen Verhältnissen in einer menschlich würdigen und angenehmen Atmosphäre. Doch ist zu bedenken, dass das nur realisiert werden kann, wo jeder einzelne seine persönlichen Interessen dem Ganzen unterordnet, dass in einer Genossenschaft alle Mitglieder die gleichen Rechte haben, dass der Vorstand keine Privilegien besitzt und kein profitgieriger (Hausmeister) ist, sondern lediglich die Interessen der Genossenschafter nach innen und aussen zu wahren hat ... So könnte eine Genossenschaft über ihren unmittelbaren Zweck hinaus Vorbild und Beispiel menschlichen Betragens und Zusammenlebens sein und ein beiden erstrebenswerten Ordnung für unsere ganze Welt.» Schön wär's.

Charlotte Peter

Die Atelierhäuser an der Wuhrstrasse im sachlichen Bauhausstil.
Fotos: Niklaus Stauss

Bücher-Hits

Folgende Bücher wurden vergangene Woche in Zürcher Buchhandlungen am häufigsten verkauft:

1. Marquez: **Die Liebe in den Zeiten der Cholera** (Kiepenheuer & Witsch, 36.60)
2. Süskind: **Die Taube** (Diogenes, 16.80)
3. Norwood: **Wenn Frauen zu sehr lieben** (Rowohlt, 27.50)
4. Kohn & Koch: **Titanic oder Arche Noah** (Rauhreif, 26.–)
5. Noll & Bachmann: **Der kleine Machiavelli** (Pendo, 24.–)
6. von Salis: **Innen und Aussen** (Orell Füssli, 48.–)
7. Wolf: **Störfall** (Luchterhand, 9.80)
8. Barnes: **New York** (Wagenbach, 27.50)
9. Muschg: **Der Turmhahn** (Suhrkamp, 25.90)
10. Canetti: **Das Geheimherz der Uhr** (Hanser, 29.50)

Die besondere Empfehlung des Buchhändlers (Stäheli):
Kohn & Koch: **Titanic oder Arche Noah** (Rauhreif, 26.–)
Im Jahre 1 nach Tschernobyl und Schweizerhalle erschien dieses Gespräch zwischen dem «starken» Mann, Michael Kohn, Schweizer Atompapst, und der «schwachen» Frau, Ursula Koch, Zürcher Stadträtin. Ein leicht verständliches Buch über grundverschiedene Weltanschauungen.

Buchhandlungen: Barth, Bodmer, Elsässer, Helvetiaplatz, Jelmoli, Nievergelt, Orell Füssli, Stäheli, Zbinden, Rennwegtor.

ANZEIGE

Willkommen auf dem Pilatus!

Auf 2132 m ü.M. Auf dem sagenumwobenen Berg mit der sagenhaft schönen Aussicht. Dort wo die Seele noch Sprünge macht.

Ab Kriens mit Gondel- und Luftseilbahn durch eines der schönsten Wandergebiete der Innerschweiz. Oder ab Alpnachstad mit der steilsten Zahnradbahn der Welt auf den Pilatusgipfel mit einladenden Restaurants und den beiden Hotels Bellevue und Pilatus-Kulm.

Chömed go luege

As I see it, there are two aspects to the developments here described as normalization of work: on one hand, they trace a path from the pathological stigmatization of creative, independent output in the nineteenth century to today's social norm, and on the other they represent the normalization of work per se. In other words, artistic work has shifted from the margins into the middle of society, while the productivity and efficiency factors of work are increasingly determining all spheres of society. Both tendencies are encountered daily in normative calls for creativity, on one hand, and effectivity, on the other. This twofold understanding of normalization means that these imperatives are already acknowledged as social norms. The mechanistic view of industrial work, as a cog in the machine, has been replaced by the self-fulfillment and creativity imperative. The artist bohemian has become obsolete, yielding to a creative and flexible enterprising self. These are, of course, ideal objectives that can never be fully achieved, which merely increases the allure, as seen particularly in the field of culture. The Wuhrstrasse flats and studios in Zurich can be considered built testimony to the distinctively modern claim to normalization and simultaneous isolation—a claim of clearly historical character in today's postindustrial Zurich under the sway of a global digital and financial environment. Aiming to achieve social integration in the context of industrial standardization may seem obsolete today, and yet there still seem to be a diversity of attempts to connect up with it. As far as societal appreciation of artistic work is concerned, it is, however, more a matter of contradictory overlapping and counter movements than of continuities: for instance, between normalization and idealization or through the mutual normalization of art and other fields of endeavor. Thus Wuhrstrasse 8/10 is not only an example, in the modern sense, of the pragmatically structured life and work of artists; it also forms a contradictory zone of different normalizations of work.

René Ed. Brauchli, *Das Atelier*, 1988: adaptation of Gustave Courbet's eponymous painting. The subjects include the Wuhrstrasse artists Valeria Stefané-Klausmann, Doris Dedual Koller, Remo Roth, Gregor, Otto Müller, Trudi Demut, and René Ed. Brauchli as well as the writer Paul Nizon

100 Jahre und kein bisschen leise

Jubiläum der Knabenschiessen-Chilbi

acl. Die Schaustellerei ist kein Honiglecken. Soviel vermag der geneigte Chilbi-Besucher zu erahnen, wenn er mit gut 800 000 Gleichgesinnten das Zürcher Knabenschiessen – in diesem Jahr vom 11. bis zum 13. September – besucht. Dass die Schausteller darüber hinaus idealistische Kulturschaffende sind, die von unersättlichen Amtsstellen an den Rand des Ruins getrieben werden, war vom Schausteller-Verband Zürich an einer Pressekonferenz beim Schützenhaus Albisgütli zu erfahren. Aus Anlass des 100-Jahr-Jubiläums der Knabenschiessen-Chilbi versicherte Jean-Pierre Hoby, Zentralsekretär der Präsidialabteilung der Stadt Zürich, den Vertretern des Schausteller-Verbandes, dass er ihre Leistung als «kulturelle Tätigkeit» schätze. Das Knabenschiessen sei neben dem Sechseläuten und der Street Parade der dritte tragende Pfeiler der Zürcher Festkultur.

Trotz dem doppelten Geburtstag – 100 Jahre Zürcher Knabenschiessen-Chilbi und 25 Jahre Schausteller-Verband Zürich – mochten die Verbandsvertreter kaum Festfreude verbreiten. Wie Vorstandsmitglied Peter Howald ausführte, leidet das Schausteller-Gewerbe unter rückläufiger Umsatzentwicklung bei steigenden Platzgebühren. Die Eintrittspreise seien mit fünf Franken am oberen Limit angelangt, während die Kosten stetig wachsen. Heute belaufe sich allein schon der Kaufpreis für eine mittelgrosse Anlage auf über eine halbe Million Franken. Zugleich werden die Schausteller zu ihrem Verdruss nicht als Kulturschaffende anerkannt und müssen deshalb die Mehrwertsteuer entrichten.

Weniger dramatisch schätzt Carlo Güntert, Platzmeister der Schützengesellschaft, die Situation ein. Gemäss seinen Aussagen sind die Platzgebühren auf dem Albisgütli-Areal seit drei Jahren unverändert. Der Betreiber einer Scooter-Bahn zahle beispielsweise 6000 Franken Miete für die drei Septembertage. Der Umsatz am Knabenschiessen übersteige jedoch 250 000 Franken. Diese Zahlen wurden von den Schaustellern zwar nicht in Abrede gestellt. Nach ihren Berechnungen bleiben von jedem erwirtschafteten Franken jedoch nur 50 Rappen in der eigenen Tasche.

Mit Tram und Auto zum geplanten Stadion Zürich

Interpellationsantwort des Stadtrates

pi. Nach heutigem Zeitplan soll das geplante multifunktionale Stadion Zürich mit Parking und Zusatznutzungen – wie der Stadtrat hofft, ein städtebaulicher Wurf mit nationaler Ausstrahlung – bis 2004/2005 fertigerstellt werden. In einer Interpellation wollte Gemeinderat Reto Dettli (sp.) wissen, wie die Verkehrserschliessung dannzumal aussehen soll. Wie der Antwort des Stadtrates zu entnehmen ist, wird die Pfingstweidstrasse mit einem Trassee für eine neue Tramlinie gemäss regionalem Richtplan ausgebaut; zudem ist eine grosszügige Baumallee vorgesehen. Diese Massnahmen sind Bestandteile eines 1997 verabschiedeten Projekts, das das kantonale Tiefbauamt unabhängig vom Entscheid zum Stadion Zürich erarbeitet hat und den Anschluss zum Stadttunnel (Hardturmstadion–Letten) sicherstellen möchte. Eine Stellungnahme der Stadt Zürich ist in Vorbereitung.

Das neue Stadion ist also direkt an das Tramnetz angebunden: einerseits an die bestehende Verbindung in der Hardturmstrasse, anderseits an die geplante neue Achse Pfingstweidstrasse–Bahnhof Altstetten. Vor der Ausführung der neuen Tramverbindung wird eine Busverbindung eingeführt, die das Sulzer-Escher-Wyss-Areal vom Bahnhof Hardbrücke via Hardstrasse–Schiffbauerstrasse–Förrlibuckstrasse–Stadion–Hardturm erschliesst. – Die Verbindung Sihlhölzli–Milchbuck (Stadttunnel) ist erst nach Fertigstellung der Westumfahrung mit dem Üetlibergtunnel (Eröffnung 2010) vorgesehen. Die Verknüpfung Pfingstweidstrasse/Hardbrücke mittels Rampen als Bestandteil des Westastes des Zürcher-Expressstrassen-Ypsilons ist im Projekt von 1997 enthalten. Der Stadtrat kann sich vorstellen, dass das neue Stadion Auslöser für eine schnelle Verwirklichung des Verkehrskonzeptes werden könnte. Für eine grundlegende Neugestaltung der Hardturmstrasse, wie dies im Stadtforum gefordert worden war, ist jedoch deren Abklassierung Voraussetzung, was eine Revision des kantonalen Richtplans verlangt. Der Stadtrat rechnet nicht damit, dass dies vor dem Ausbau der Pfingstweidstrasse der Fall sein könnte.

Passant in Zürich 4 beraubt

Überfall um 3 Uhr nachts

tom. Ein 42jähriger Mann ist in der Nacht auf Donnerstag, kurz nach 3 Uhr, an der Hohlstrasse in Zürich 4, nach dem Verlassen einer Bar überfallen worden. Drei unbekannte Männer traten – laut Stadtpolizei – von hinten an ihn heran und hielten ihn fest. Sie streiften dem Opfer eine wertvolle Armbanduhr vom Handgelenk und entwendeten ihm das Portemonnaie. Anschliessend flüchteten sie mit der Beute von mehreren tausend Franken. Einer der Täter wird als schlanker, etwa 170 Zentimeter grosser Mann mit kurz geschorenen, schwarzen Haaren beschrieben. Er trug ein weisses T-Shirt und dunkle Jeans. Die beiden Komplizen waren dunkel gekleidet. Allfällige Hinweise sind an die Stadtpolizei Zürich, Telefon (01) 216 71 11, erbeten.

Atelierhaus mit ungebrochener Ausstrahlung

Ein Baudenkmal von Ernst Gisel an der Wuhrstrasse

S. K. Manche Häuser wirken schon kurz nach ihrem Bau überholt, schlecht geplant und ausgeführt. Andere wiederum setzen erst mit den Jahren Patina an und erhalten einen gewissen Charme. Es gibt aber auch Häuser, die stehen von Anfang an wie unverrückbare Denkmäler an ihrem Platz, überzeugen im Äussern wie im Innern und fügen sich harmonisch in ihre Umgebung ein. Ein solches Haus ist das 1949 geplante und drei Jahre später erbaute Atelierhaus von Ernst Gisel für die Baugenossenschaft Maler und Bildhauer an der Wuhrstrasse 8 und 10 in Zürich Wiedikon. Seit den frühen fünfziger Jahren erfüllt der unprätentiöse, gradlinig ernsthafte Backsteinbau mit dem stimmungsvollen Ateliertrakt und dem ummauerten Skulpturenhof dieselbe Funktion, nämlich Wohn- und Arbeitsort für Maler und Bildhauer zu sein.

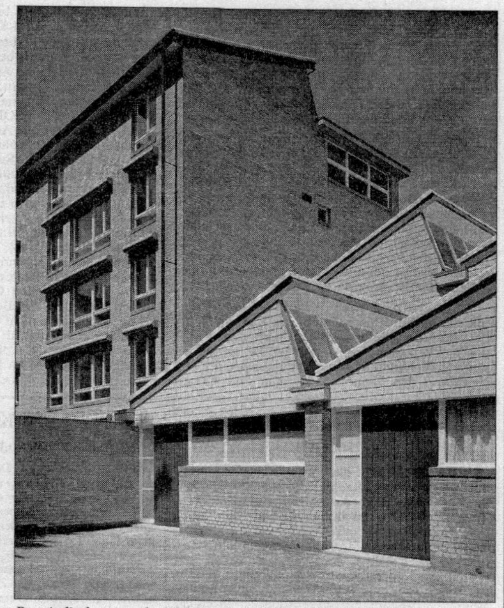

Das Atelierhaus an der Wuhrstrasse mit dem Skulpturenhof und den Anbauten für Bildhauerateliers. (Bild Walter Binder)

Viele Häuser in Zürich, in denen Künstler während und nach dem Zweiten Weltkrieg provisorisch ihre Ateliers eingerichtet hatten, wurden in den Wirtschaftswunder-Jahren abgebrochen, so dass die Künstler immer wieder buchstäblich auf der Strasse standen. So schlossen sich drei von ihnen – der Maler Max Truninger und die beiden Bildhauer Otto Müller und Otto Teucher – 1949 zusammen und gründeten die Baugenossenschaft Maler und Bildhauer Zürich.

Mit ihrer Idee des Künstler-Atelierhauses fanden sie beim befreundeten Architekten Ernst Gisel offene Ohren, hatte dieser doch bereits 1947 in Zumikon ein Wohn- und Arbeitshaus für Hans Aeschbach gebaut, das der Graphiker und Maler bis zu seinem Tod im Frühjahr 1999 bewohnte. Später kam am gleichen Ort im Auftrag eines deutschen Fabrikanten ein Dreieratelierhaus hinzu, das neben dem Bauherrn der Architekt selbst und der Künstler Walter Sauter bewohnten. Der Entwurf für das Haus an der Wuhrstrasse mit zwölf Ateliers und acht Wohnungen folgte einem Idealplan für Künstlerhäuser, den der Architekt im Auftrag der Stadt Zürich für ein Grundstück an der Dufourstrasse ausgearbeitet hatte. Das Projekt liess sich indes am vorgesehenen Standort im Seefeld nicht realisieren, die Stadt überliess der Baugenossenschaft deshalb ein knapp 1300 m² grosses Grundstück an der Wuhrstrasse im Baurecht für die Dauer von achtzig Jahren.

Im Juli 1952 war Baubeginn, und im März des folgenden Jahres wurden die ersten Ateliers bezogen. Zu den prominentesten Bewohnern in der Anfangszeit des Atelierhauses gehörten die Bildhauer Hans Aeschbacher, Otto Teucher und Otto Müller, die Maler Friedrich Kuhn, Carlotta Stokker und Carlo Vivarelli. Auch Silvio Mattioli und Bert Schmidmeister wohnten zeitweise an der Wuhrstrasse.

In seinem Äussern wie im Innern strahlt das fünfgeschossige Backsteingebäude mit dem Atelieranbau eine schlichte Eleganz aus. Im Attikageschoss des Wohntraktes sind zusätzlich vier Ateliers untergebracht, eine Idee, die der Architekt auch in anderen Mehrfamilienhäusern verwirklichte. Ein gedeckter Laubengang führt zu den Malerateliers im Rückgebäude, die Bildhauerateliers liegen etwas zurückgestaffelt und haben einen direkten Zugang zum Hof, der die Möglichkeit zur Arbeit im Freien bietet. Eine einfache Betonmauer mit einem Tor gegen die Strasse schliesst diesen gegen die Nachbarhäuser ab und betont den Werkcharakter des Aussenraumes.

Oberlichter in den Einschnitten der Sheddächer und ein seitliches Fensterband erhellen die unterschiedlich hohen, meist weiss getünchten Ateliers. Der hauptsächliche Lichteinfall von Nordosten oder Nordwesten bietet gute Arbeitsbedingungen, wird doch das helle Nordlicht von den Künstlern besonders geschätzt. Die relativ kleinen Dreizimmerwohnungen sind in ihrer Einteilung und Ausstattung seit den Anfängen praktisch unverändert geblieben. Die heutigen Bewohner setzen sich für eine möglichst originale Erhaltung der vom Architekten gestalteten Klinker- und Parkettböden, der rohen oder weiss verputzten Backsteinwände, der Wandschränke, Raumunterteilungen mittels Schiebetüren und der vergleichsweise spartanischen Küchenausstattungen ein. Das alte Steingutspülbecken erfüllt dort ebenso noch seinen Zweck wie die verschiedenen hölzernen Ablagen, so dass auf den Einbau moderner Küchenkombinationen verzichtet werden konnte. Einzig die Bäder wurden teilweise neu gestaltet. Die hohen, die ganze Wandbreite einnehmenden Fenster mit ihrer Unterteilung in Kipp- und Flügelfenster unterstreichen den Werkstattcharakter des Gebäudes. Die charakteristischen, sich darüber wölbenden blechernen Rolladenkästen mussten vor einiger Zeit ausgewechselt werden, ebenso wie die Eternitabdeckung des Daches. Die original hölzernen Rolläden wurden dabei durch solche aus Metall ersetzt.

Der Genossenschaftsgedanke unter den Mitgliedern, die ihr Atelierhaus selbst verwalten, funktioniert bis heute. Die schlichten, karg ausgestatteten Räume vermochten indes manche der arrivierteren Künstler nicht zu halten, wie Architekt Ernst Gisel bemerkt.

Der linksalternative Kandidat

Niklaus Scherr zieht es nach Bern

mbm. Über seine Chancen, als Ständerat nach Bern gewählt zu werden, macht sich der 55jährige Niklaus Scherr, Zürcher Gemeinderat der Alternativen Liste (AL) und Geschäftsleiter des Zürcher Mieterverbands, keine Illusionen. Wie er am Donnerstag an einer Pressekonferenz in Zürich erklärt hat, strebt er an, die beiden bisherigen und wiederkandidierenden Ständeräte, Vreni Spoerry (fdp.) und Hans Hofmann (svp.), mit der Unterstützung der drei links-grünen Kandidatinnen in einen zweiten Wahlgang zu zwingen. Mit seiner Kandidatur möchte er den Wahlberechtigten eine soziale und urbane Alternative anbieten. Es gehe nicht an, dass Zürich im Ständerat von einem «Exponenten der Blocher-Partei» und von einer «Vertreterin der Hochfinanz» repräsentiert werde.

Scherr, der engagierte, linksalternative Lokalpolitiker, stellte ein Programm mit sechs Schwerpunkten vor. Demnach will er sich als Ständerat energisch gegen die Demontage des Mietrechts und gegen die weitere Privatisierung von Staatsbetrieben einsetzen. Ein besonders Anliegen seien ihm auch ein bezahlbares Gesundheitswesen und die Sicherung der AHV sowie der IV; die Krankenkassenprämien müssten von Einkommen und Vermögen abhängig gemacht werden. Ferner befürwortet Scherr die Drogenlegalisierung und den Uno-Beitritt. Grundsätzlich ist er für eine aktive und solidarische Aussenpolitik wie auch für eine weltoffene und tolerante Schweiz, die sich damit abfindet, ein Einwanderungsland zu sein.

Trotz geringen Chancen in der Ständeratswahl ist der seit mehr als 20 Jahren in der Lokalpolitik aktive Scherr zuversichtlich, den Sprung nach Bern zu schaffen: Er ist Spitzenkandidat auf der Nationalratsliste der AL, die mit der SP und der GP Listenverbindungen eingegangen ist. Eine allfällige Wahl nach Bern würde, so liess Scherr verlauten, das Ende seiner Karriere als Gemeinderat bedeuten. Im Ständeratswahlkampf wird Scherr von einem Komitee unterstützt, dem auch Stadträtin Monika Stocker angehört. An der Pressekonferenz bezeichnete Susanne Erdös, Vizepräsidentin der SP der Stadt Zürich und Gemeinderätin, Niklaus Scherr als messerscharfen Denker und geschickten Politstrategen, der sich durch Beharrlichkeit, Kompetenz, Witz und Biss auszeichne.

Politsplitter

Kreis 2 – guter Boden für Politfrauen

sir. Die an sich erfreuliche Mitteilung hat auch eine unerfreuliche Komponente: Gemeinderat Jürg Liebermann (fdp., Zürich 2), ein aufgeschlossener, hochanständiger Parlamentarier, Mitglied der Rechnungsprüfungskommission, von Beruf Wirtschaftsprüfer und mit jener Kompetenz ausgestattet, von der FDP und Gemeinderat noch mehr brauchen könnten, tritt aus persönlich-beruflichen Gründen auf den 22. September zurück. Das ist bedauerlich! – Seine Nachfolge antreten wird Therese Hensch-Stadelmann, womit die bürgerliche Frauendelegation des Stadtkreises 2 auf sage und schreibe 5 Gemeinderätinnen wächst, die gesamte Frauendelegation auf deren 7. Von den 10 Ratsmitgliedern von Zürich 2 gehören deren 2 der SVP an, nämlich Beatrix Casutt und Raphaela-Franziska Ulcay-Hauser. Die künftige FDP-2-Gemeinderatsdelegation setzt sich zusammen aus: Andrea Widmer Graf, Caroline Rom-Bernheim, Therese Hensch-Stadelmann und – dem anscheinend unvermeidlichen Mann – Urs Lauffer. Die Sozialdemokraten sind, wie es sich für eine eher konservative Partei gehört, ausgewogen zusammengesetzt. Ihre vier Sitze werden von zwei Damen und zwei Herren eingenommen, nämlich von Anna Brändle Galliker, von Fiammetta Jahreiss-Montagnani, von Reto Heygel und von Benjamin Naef.

In Kürze

«Städtische» wollen Teuerungsausgleich

ese. Der VPOD Zürich Städtische, die grösste Gewerkschaft des städtischen Personals, fordert vom Stadtrat den Teuerungsausgleich für alle städtischen Arbeitnehmer. Die Löhne seien letztmals per Januar 1996 auf einem Indexstand von 102,2 Punkten angepasst worden, heisst es in einer Mitteilung. Bis im Juli 1999 habe sich damit ein Rückstand von 1,3 Prozent ergeben. Der VPOD verlangt nun auf den 1. Januar 2000 den vollen Ausgleich der Teuerung. – Die Forderung fällt mitten in die Beratungen des Stadtrats zum Budget 2000. Offenbar will die Gewerkschaft mit dem Communiqué den Druck auf den Stadtrat erhöhen.

Bauarbeiten in der Weinbergstrasse

c. Die bald hundertjährigen Kanäle und Wasserleitungen in der Weinbergstrasse zwischen Leonhard- und Sonneggstrasse müssen erneuert werden. Auch die Tramgeleise im Bereich der Haltestelle Haldenegg sind stark abgenützt und müssen ersetzt werden. Die entsprechenden Bauarbeiten beginnen am Montag.

VON TAG ZU TAG

Schachgrossmeister Wladimir Kramnik in Zürich. Die in Zürich ansässige Stiftung «Fonds zur Förderung des Jugendschachs in der Schweiz» feiert an diesem Wochenende ihren 25. Geburtstag. Höhepunkt der Feierlichkeiten ist ein Uhrensimultan des russischen Grossmeisters Wladimir Kramnik, der aktuellen Nr. 3 der Weltrangliste, gegen eine verjüngte Schweizer Nationalmannschaft. Dabei spielt Kramnik gleichzeitig gegen sechs Nationalspieler. Die Partien beginnen heute um 16 Uhr und können bis zu sechseinhalb Stunden dauern. Für Zuschauer ist der Eintritt gratis. Die Partien können direkt oder in einem Nebenraum, wo sie von einem Meisterspieler kommentiert werden, verfolgt werden. Schauplatz des Spektakels ist das Hotel Savoy Baur en Ville am Paradeplatz. *lub.*

Messen für Hausbesitzer ... und Leute, die es werden wollen finden seit gestern Donnerstag auf dem Messegelände in Zürich Oerlikon statt. In den neuen Messehallen zeigen 500 Aussteller ihre Dienstleistungen und Produkte im Zusammenhang mit der Sanierung von Altbauten. Die Messe dauert bis Montag und ist von 9 bis 18 Uhr geöffnet. Nebenan, im Stadthof 11, führen die Zürcher Kantonalbank und die Oerlikon-Bührle Immobilien AG die «Immobilia» durch, eine «überregionale Messe für Wohneigentum». Die Messe dauert bis Sonntag und ist am Freitag von 16 bis 20 Uhr geöffnet, samstags und sonntags von 10 bis 17 Uhr. *ese.*

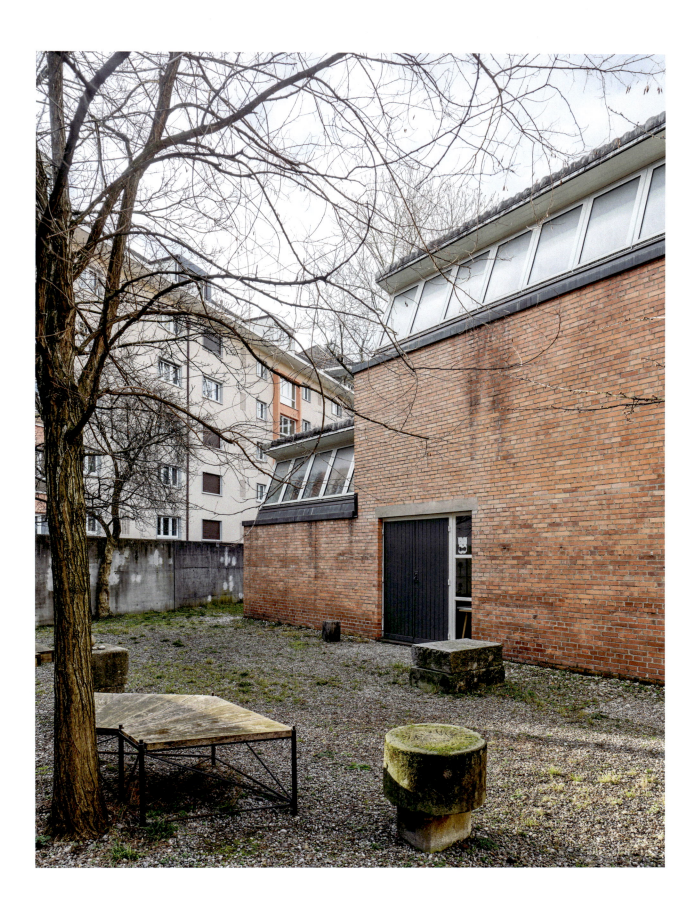

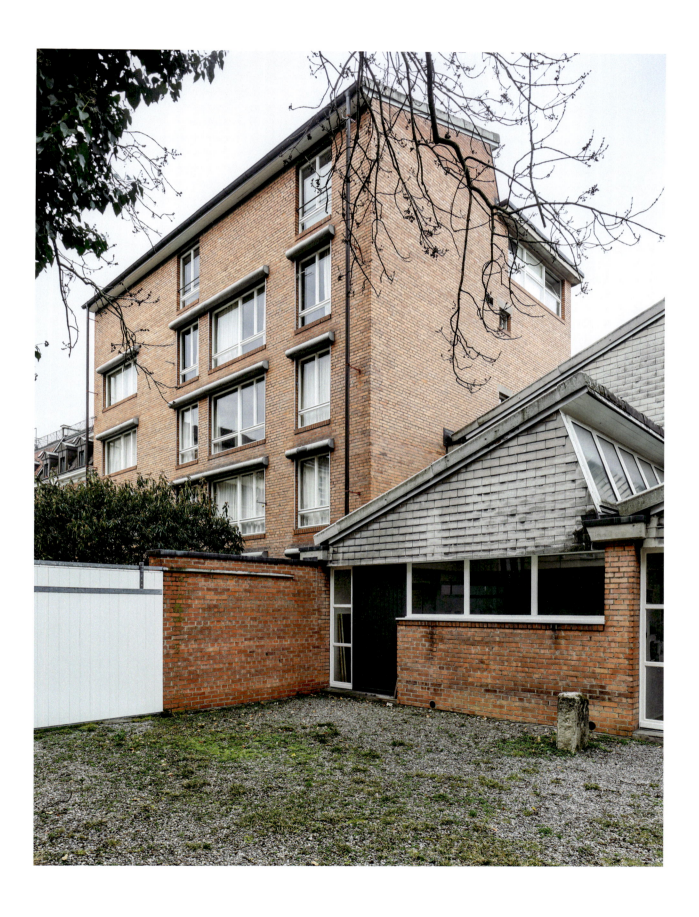

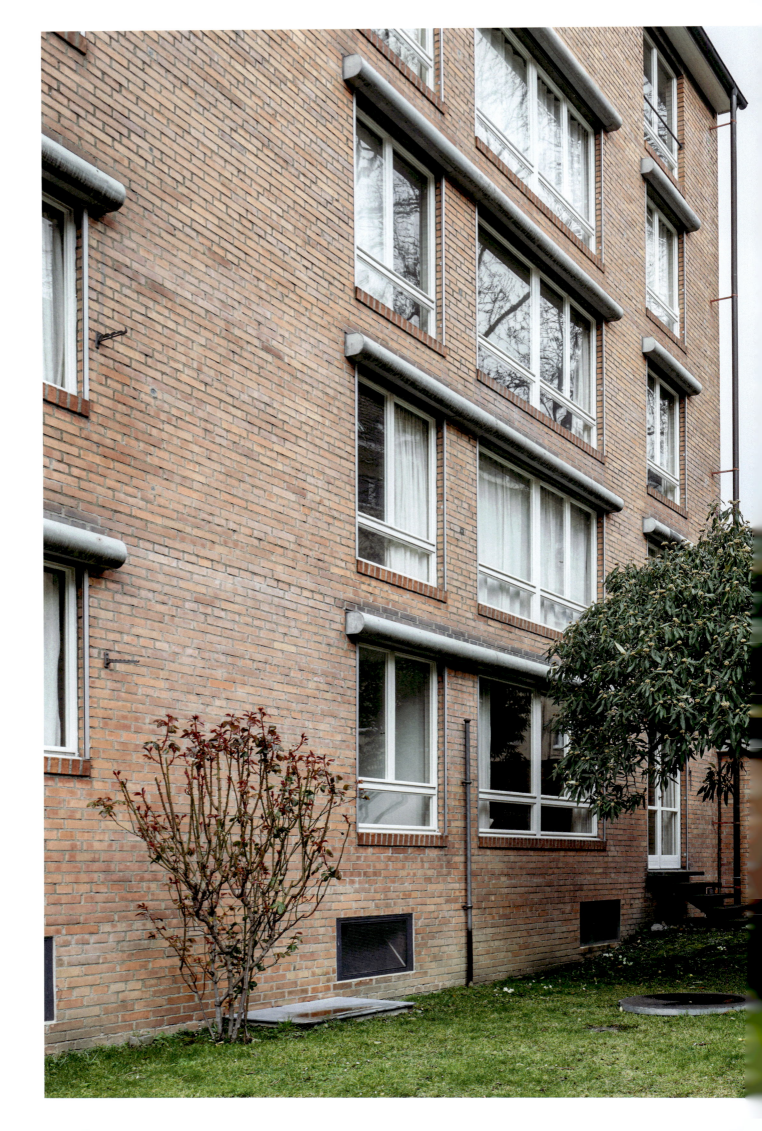

At the entrance to Otto Müller's studio, c. 1990

"WUHRSTRASSE" AND ITS REACH— A CHRONICLE

GABRIELLE SCHAAD

Close to seventy years ago, the the Painters and Sculptors Building Cooperative Zurich was erected at Wuhrstrasse as a model with a future. Now we look back and wonder: how are history, art history, and biographies along with anecdotes by decades of artists residing at Wuhrstrasse interwoven into a contextualized history that extends into the present day? Where in Zurich and beyond did the residents make an impact and, at times, provoke controversy? When did they work with or against the (Zurich) zeitgeist? A look back and into the studios of the "Wuhrstrasse colony" situates the artists against the background of seven decades of current trends and events. A closer look at the activities of members of the cooperative from different generations, and with varying degrees of fame and influence, reveals how the image of the artist, working conditions, and exhibitions have changed over the years. The "chronicle" presented here is by nature selective and lays no claim to being complete.

1950S: BETWEEN "CLARTÉ FRANÇAISE" AND "NEW GRAPHIC ART"

When the members of the cooperative moved into the new building at Wuhrstrasse 8/10 in 1953, the young architect Max Frisch, just back from the United States, critically pitted the "moderation" and "neighborliness" characteristic of Swiss housing against the diametrically opposed ideal of life as an urban "nomad."[1] Grateful to have a roof over their heads, the artists at Wuhrstrasse had more existential concerns to deal with. "Artists were poor more often than they are today, poor as church mice," writer Urs Widmer recalls at a symposium in 2009 on the "Expansion of Modernism" in the "muted" 1950s in Switzerland.[2] Here, as in the new consumer societies nearby, the standard of living was rapidly rising; social security or the AHV, as it was called in Switzerland, had already been introduced in 1948. However, for artists, the prospects of a place to live and security in old age had not seen much improvement. The Baugenossenschaft Maler und Bildhauer Zürich (the Painters and Sculptors Building Cooperative Zurich), established in 1949, alongside the Zürcher Baugenossenschaft für Künstler-Ateliers (Zurich Building Cooperative for Artists' Studios), which ensured temporary quarters for artists in a canton-owned building on Südstrasse, offered an unprecedented opportunity. The shortage of workspace and often precarious living conditions of artists found relief in the concrete measure of a cooperative studio-cum-residential building at Wuhrstrasse designed by Ernst Gisel.

Although the artists who moved in now had the security of a roof over their heads, many of them still had their sights set on Paris. In Zurich, Café Select and Café Odeon were substitutes of sorts as literary cafés where people in the arts could gather and discuss the latest trends. But it was in Paris, in 1953, that the Théâtre Babylone premiered Samuel Beckett's *Waiting for Godot*—in retrospect, perhaps symbolic of the postwar excitement and anticipation of new developments that were initially somewhat slow to take off in Switzerland.[3] In 1955, in the catalogue for the third edition of the exhibition *Tendances actuelles* at Kunsthalle Bern, curator Arnold Rüdlinger succinctly situated the art historical trends of the decade and, within it, the role of Wuhrstrasse, suggesting that orientation toward Paris had become obsolete because of polycentric art activities and, not least, the tachist trajectory of art practitioners in Switzerland.

Nonetheless, the halo over Paris lost none of its shine until the early 1960s—least of all in Switzerland. Unperturbed by Rüdlinger's diagnosis, Wuhrstrasse resident Henri Wengér, dealer in art and antiquities, continued to build bridges to Paris. He ran the Librairie Française not far from Kunsthaus Zürich between 1944 and 1957, an antiquarian shop for books and original prints, which became a meeting place and "party cellar" for his illustrious circle of friends, among them, Jean Cocteau, Fernand Léger, Paul Valéry, and Eugène Ionesco. (FIG. 1) In the early 1960s, Wengér expanded the antiquarian bookshop, so popular among international and local artists and writers, into a gallery that he installed

---

[1] Max Frisch, "Cum grano salis. Eine kleine Glosse zur schweizerischen Architektur," in *Werk*, 40, (1953), pp. 325–329, p. 325.

[2] Urs Widmer, "Aufbruch aus dem Dumpfen" in *Expansion der Moderne. Wirtschaftswunder—Kalter Krieg—Avantgarde—Populärkultur*, outlines 5, SIK-ISEA, eds. Juerg Albrecht et al., Zurich, 2010, p. 14.

[3] Jakob Tanner, "Die Schweiz in den 50er-Jahren, blockiert zwischen Vorgestern und Übermorgen," in *Kulturmagazin* 57, June/July (1986), pp. 8–15.

FIG. 1 Henri Wengér in lively conversation with Jean Cocteau. The listeners are the stars of Cocteau's film *Les Enfants Terribles*, Nicole Stéphane and Edouard Dermite, who were in Zurich on the occasion of a French cinema week at Nord-Süd movie theater, and artist Jeannie Borel in the center, Librairie Française, Zurich, March 1950

FIG. 2 Henri Wengér in his gallery, mid-1960s

FIG. 3 Artist and art dealer Silvio R. Baviera (left) and curator Harald Szeemann (right), preview, Galerie Henri Wengér, c. 1970

at his new location on Neumarkt 1 until 1972. (FIGS. 2+3) In 1957, the *Neue Zürcher Zeitung* wrote about the move—or rather about the newly established Henri Wengér Gallery—with then typically Francophile undertones: "The small shop [...] shows that 'clarté française' [...] with which its proprietor interweaves his love of art and his remarks on artists."[4]

At Galerie Wengér, we also pick up the trail of Tildy Grob, whom her friends lovingly dubbed "Pierrot." She was a crucial protagonist in the early years, inasmuch as the vanishing lines of art and contemporary events intersect in her work. A native of Winterthur, she had studied at the Art Academy in Hamburg. In the early 1950s, she stopped in at Wengér's Librairie Française in Zurich to inquire whether she might present her works in his shop. She ended up with a job there and later went on to work in her future husband's gallery as well. In 1953 the couple moved into the cooperative and as of 1955 Tildy Grob-Wengér also rented a studio there. Numerous anecdotes circulate about her contact with the doyens of art and literature in Paris between antiquarian shop, art gallery, and studio. While at the Parisian studio La Courrière, she befriended Marc Chagall and Max Ernst and studied etching.

The name Picasso continued to figure in Tildy Grob-Wengér's life beyond the prints on sale at Galerie Wengér. The Swiss *Stiftung für die Graphische Kunst* (Foundation of Graphic Arts) awarded her in 1976 the "Prix Picasso" for her work on paper and she received CHF 3000 from an endowment Picasso made to the Print Collection of the ETH Zürich. Before moving into the Wuhrstrasse studio, Tildy Grob had already become familiar, in her capacity as a sculptor, with socially committed representatives of postwar modernist architecture in Switzerland. She modeled a series of portraits and sculptures of children for the Pestalozzi Children's Village built in 1949 in Trogen by architect and artist Hans Fischli.[5] When professionals criticized Fischli's gabled roofs in the philanthropic settlement, calling it a "toy village" in "chalet style," he retorted that the angle of a roof does not define modern, contemporary architecture.[6] Nonetheless, after making the sculptures of children for Trogen, Tildy Grob increasingly took a turn toward semi-figurative representation and abstraction in her prints and paintings. Her contributions to print biennials also garnered international acclaim.

In 1958 she contributed to SAFFA, *Schweizerische Ausstellung für Frauenarbeit* (Swiss Exhibition of Women's Work) as "a specialist for sculptural tasks." This "national women's exhibition" was mounted in the run-up to the referendum on giving women the right to vote, which had failed in 1947. SAFFA attracted almost two million visitors to the pavilions at and on Lake Zurich designed by such architects as Lisbeth Sachs and Annemarie Hubacher-Constam. Grob-Wengér attracted attention with the modular, abstract/geometric display systems that she created for the "fashion carousel." (FIG. 4) The exhibition brochure praised not only her designs for SAFFA and the MUBA trade fair in Basel, but also her wide-ranging expertise in working with "plaster mesh, papier-mâché, and polyester casts of exceptionally light execution."[7]

In addition to Grob-Wengér, another Wuhrstrasse studio resident, the painter Carlotta Stocker, made a prominently placed contribution to SAFFA with her figurative mural *Innerschweiz* (1958).[8] Stocker later wrote: "Having grown up in Zurich, I found my childhood memories of holidays in the canton of Uri quite helpful [...]: I was deeply impressed by the hard life there and the battle with nature. But I couldn't forget the contrast with the loving warmth radiated by the small sky-blue madonnas [there]. We didn't have a higher 'image' of womanhood."[9] In her provocative, progressive pamphlet, *Frauen im Laufgitter* (Women in the Playpen), written in 1958 on the occasion of SAFFA, innovative feminist thinker Iris von Roten explicitly noted the structural disadvantages that women suffered with regard to work, self-determined sexuality, and political participation. Significantly, neither Grob-Wengér nor Stocker bowed to the restrictions and conventions still prevalent in the 1950s, but it is worthy of note that in the

---

4 "Galerie Henri Wengér," *Neue Zürcher Zeitung*, Dec. 16, 1957, p. 16.
5 See Archive Holdings SIK-ISEA, Tildy Grob-Wengér artist's dossier.
6 Hans Fischli, "Das Kinderdorf Pestalozzi in Trogen: erbaut und dargestellt von Arch. H. Fischli," in *Schweizerische Bauzeitung*, vol. 67, no. 45, (1949), pp. 637–642.
7 See Archive Holdings SIK-ISEA, Tildy Grob-Wengér artist's dossier.
8 See Archive Holdings SIK-ISEA, Carlotta Stocker artist's dossier.
9 Carlotta Stocker, "Die Kunstwerke im Schulhaus Wipkingerbrücke." Correspondence in: Archive Holdings SIK-ISEA, Carlotta Stocker artist's dossier.

same decade, there were thirteen men and four women residing at Wuhrstrasse. Carlo Vivarelli, also a member of the cooperative, represented the movement of Concrete artists in Zurich, although, when he joined in 1953—the same year that "die gute Form" (good form) became a Swiss registered trademark—he was welcomed as a celebrated commercial artist and designer. He created articles of daily use in the spirit of "good" design with the intention of cultivating the good taste of users, echoing the fact that the social function of visual information underpinned his work ethic and aesthetics. Through the *Flums Grossberg* poster campaign (1940), Vivarelli chalked up early success as a pioneer of photography and photomontage alongside Herbert Matter. Between 1958 and 1965, Vivarelli worked from his "base" at Wuhrstrasse with the designers Richard Paul Lohse, Hans Neuburg, and Josef Müller-Brockmann in the editorial collective of the journal *Neue Grafik*. The celebrated designer Müller-Brockmann initiated the *Internationale Zeitschrift für Grafik-Design und verwandte Themen* on the margins of their shared participation in the exhibition *Konstruktive Grafik* (1958) at the Kunstgewerbemuseum Zürich and Vivarelli was responsible, among other things, for the design of the magazine cover.

Carlo Vivarelli's contribution to visual communication influenced the discourse on design far beyond Wuhrstrasse; his work also exerted an influence on everyday life in domestic living rooms and kitchens—for instance, his design of the Swiss TV logo that flickered across screens day after day in all three language regions between 1958 and 1985, with the cropped leg of the T running parallel to the V, (FIG. 5) or the clean design of the Electrolux logo, still in use today, with its geometrically reduced allusion to the letter E. (FIG. 6) In addition, between 1953 and 1963, Vivarelli was design consultant for Feller AG in Horgen and Therma AG, (FIG. 7) both specialized in the installation of electricity for (private) households. It was not until the 1960s that the designer gradually abandoned his diverse commissions in commercial design to devote himself entirely to his art. In 1977, as a member of the art commission, he contributed to the design of the new university campus at Zurich-Irchel, and from 1978 to 1986 he was on the board of the Zurich Art Society. In his lifetime, however, Vivarelli's concrete sculptures in public space met with a somewhat lukewarm reception. The sculpture *Fünfteilige Säule aus 10 identischen Gruppen* (Five-Part Column of 10 Identical Groups, 1967–69) that still crowns the terrace of the University cafeteria had long been dubbed the "Hunger Tower" in response to the sparing, low-key aesthetic of Concrete art. (FIG. 8) And so, in the early days of the Wuhrstrasse, figurative-abstract sculptors coexisted with painters, practitioners of arts and crafts, and Constructive-Concrete graphic artists.

FIG. 4   Tildy Grob-Wengér, *Modekarusell*, pavilion for *SAFFA 1958* (Swiss Exhibition of Women's Work), Zurich, 1958

FIG. 5   Carlo Vivarelli, Logo for Swiss television (in use from 1958 to 1985), 1958

FIG. 6   Carlo Vivarelli, logo for Electrolux, 1961

Carlo Vivarelli, logo for Lascaux, Swiss maker of paints and pigments, 1957

FIG. 7   Carlo Vivarelli, logo for Therma, 1958

1960S AND 1970S: ON POPULARIZATION AND POLITICS

"The end of 'good form' as a touring exhibition of the Swiss Werkbund coincided with the cultural revolution,"[10] art historian Kornelia Imesch writes in reference to the year 1968. Interestingly, there was room for a diversity of artistic approaches in the cooperative at Wuhrstrasse. There was no need to initiate a "cultural revolution"; it was already there, for instance, in the work of Friedrich Kuhn.

Kuhn presented his paintings, prints, and sculptures essentially to counter the unyielding fronts of both gestural abstraction and Constructivist-Concrete art, as embodied, from the 1960s, in the form of a palm tree in front of the "overfurnished"[11] interiors that characterize his late work, or in the form of freestanding wooden sculptures on consoles. In 1964, the national exhibition *Expo 64* in Lausanne provoked heated debate. Writers like Marxist critic Konrad Farner or architect and writer Max Frisch described the projected self-image of the national state as "Delusion Switzerland."[12] It is therefore hardly surprising that Friedrich Kuhn's contribution to the Expo 64 for the pavilion "Modern Switzerland," designed in collaboration with Zurich painter Varlin, showed an ironic interpretation of a foundering Switzerland in a gigantic, gloomy blue panorama. (FIG. 9) Varlin did not paint his *Heilsarmee* (Salvation Army) and *Völlerei* (Gluttony), 1964, at Wuhrstrasse but rather in a studio on Neumarkt that the city of Zurich had provided for him in 1958.

In 1968, art historian and writer Paul Nizon, who was closely associated with Kuhn and the residence at Wuhrstrasse, summed up the situation in his frequently cited essay for the *Zürcher Almanach*, 1968, titled "Zürcher Schule der Kleinen Wahnwelt" (Zurich School of Minor Madness).[13] A print created by Kuhn was prominently featured in the almanac. In his title, Nizon was referring to a group of artists around Kuhn and Fred Engelbert Knecht, who, as he writes, not only aimed to criticize, change, and revolutionize the reality of modern life in Zurich, but negated and opted out of it entirely, instead setting up and settling down in their own antithetical dream reality of the faraway and the fantastic, from the macabre to the naïve.[14] While the work of the artists immortalized by Nizon invented and projected alternative realities as places of refuge, the next generation was already moving forward with the aim of transformation in real life, by establishing spaces specifically for young people through projects such as the autonomous youth center (AJZ).

The demands of this younger generation for space of their own culminated on June 29/30, 1968 in the notorious, police-dominated protests in front of the temporary Globus department store on the Bahnhofbrücke, which have gone down in history as the "Globus Riots." Historians Erika Hebeisen and Elisabeth Joris recall that, despite continuing calls for independent spaces for (youth) culture, "nonconformist" practitioners created numerous new locations between 1964 and 1968 beyond the cooperative at Wuhrstrasse.[15] An open space for happenings was established, for instance, at Club Platte[nstrasse 27] and in 1966 musician Hardy Hepp founded the Zürcher Kommune at Hechtplatz 1 between Café Select and Café Odeon.

On the whole the (student) protests of 1968, with their demand for renewal and change, may have been less explosive in Switzerland than elsewhere, unfolding gradually, but they did initiate profound change in the teaching of art. Hansjörg Mattmüller, a protagonist of this progressive transformation that had already been making inroads since the mid-1960s, moved into an apartment studio at Wuhrstrasse in the early 1970s. In 1958, architect and artist Hans Fischli, dean and director of the Kunstgewerbemuseum until 1961, had appointed him head of the preparatory course at the Zurich School of Applied Arts, where he worked alongside cofounder and resident of the cooperative Otto Teucher and had contact with Hans Finsler and Elsi Giauque.

FIG. 8 Carlo Vivarelli, concrete sculpture *-teilige Säule aus 10 identischen Gruppen*, cafeteria terrace, University of Zurich, c. 1969

FIG. 9 Friedrich Kuhn, *Rêve helvétique (la nté)* and *Rêve helvétique*, mural paintings for *EXPO 64*, 64

Kornelia Imesch, "'Gute Form' und lter Krieg.' Die Schweizer Filmwochenschau: Bill'sche ik der Ästhetik aus Funktion und als Funktion," in *Ex- sion der Moderne*, eds. Juerg Albrecht, et al. (see note ove), p. 156.

11 Paul Nizon, *Friedrich Kuhn [eine Monographie]*, Verlag Um die Ecke, Zurich, 1969.
12 Ueli Mäder, *68 – was bleibt?*, Rotpunktverlag, Zurich, 2018, p. 21
13 Paul Nizon, "Zürcher Schule der Kleinen Wahnwelt," in *Zürcher Almanach*, Benziger, Zurich/Einsiedeln/Cologne, 1968, pp. 79–90.

14 Ibid.
15 Erika Hebeisen, Elisabeth Joris, Angela Zimmermann, eds., *Zürich 68: Kollektive Aufbrüche ins Ungewisse*, hier + jetzt, Baden, 2008.

FIG. 10 Hansjörg Mattmüller, artists and patrons Doris Stauffer and Serge Stauffer with painter Bendicht Fivian (latter two in front) on the roof of the Kunstgewerbeschule Zürich, after having founded the independent F+F school of art as an offshoot of the *Klasse F+F* in March 1970

FIG. 11 Invitation of the Produzentengalerie Zürich (PRODUGA) for the exhibition in the Arte Arena Gallery, Zurich, 1973
Group photograph by Roland Gretler of members of PRODUGA (including René Ed. Brauchli and Remo Roth), posing with the tools of their trade, winter 1972/73

However, crucial impetus for reform came from cofounder Mattmüller in 1965, within the framework of the class "Form und Farbe" (F+F, form and color). Working together with the experimental art pedagogue Doris Stauffer, her husband, the Duchamp specialist and art historian Serge Stauffer, as well as Bendicht Fivian, (FIG. 10) Peter Gygax, and Peter Jenny, he moved beyond conventional painting classes and the grip of functionally defined "design," not only introducing a nonhierarchical, participative art curriculum, but also modifying the content of the courses and their format to tie in with contemporary international developments in such fields as Land Art, process art, performance, and media art. In 1969, when Doris Stauffer took a student's suggestion and introduced a course in "teamwork," the smoldering conflict with city authorities, the school administration, and the student council came to a head. In 1970, students and teachers, including Mattmüller, submitted "written notice" to the new administration under Mark Buchmann, citing "unacceptable conditions at the KGSZ." After their classes were disbanded, they incorporated their radical, pedagogical teaching plan in 1971 into a new organization, the F+F Schule für Informationsgestaltung (F+F School of Information Design), which still exists today as the privately run F+F Kunstschule.

The radical teaching methods introduced in the "form and color" class, which would later become the F+F Kunstschule, seminally influenced an upcoming generation of artists.[16] Mattmüller came into his own as a teacher but never ceased working in his Wuhrstrasse studio on his own art, on his whimsically bizarre drawings and zestful calligraphy.[17] He also brought a fresh wind to Wuhrstrasse by introducing younger artists, like Peter Trachsel (aka Hasena), who was a student of the performance class at the F+F. Peter Stiefel, still assistant to Friedrich Kuhn in 1972, worked at the cooperative from 1982–1989, while Alesch Vital, then experimenting with polyester sculptures and performance, was a familiar face as the assistant of Silvio Mattioli. René Ed. Brauchli, a member of the Wuhrstrasse cooperative from 1965 to 2005, is said to have been so fascinated the first time he visited sculptor Otto Müller's studio in the 1960s that he transformed his "awakening" into an angel drawn on the wall of Müller's studio.

"In the fall of 1972, a group of artists, critics, and art lovers from Zurich founded the gallery collective *PRODUGA (Produzentengalerie/* Producers' *Gallery)*. The gallery originated in the fine arts special committee of the GKEW (*Gewerkschaft für Kultur, Erziehung und Wissenschaft/* Union for Culture, Education, and Science), established in the late 1960s. Many members of *PRODUGA* had already been active in Zurich in the 1968 movement, some of them involved in the youth section of the PdA (*Partei der Arbeit/* Party of Labor) or in the Zurich Manifesto, formed in the summer of 1968."[18] René Ed. Brauchli, Remo Roth, and Werner W. Wyss were closely associated with *PRODUGA* and contributed, along with the politically motivated collective, to their first group exhibition *Wir Bildermacher arbeiten hier und jetzt* (We Picture Makers Work Here and Now) at the Galerie Arte Arena in Dübendorf in 1973. (FIG. 11) The well-established artists Otto Müller and Trudi Demut—both committed Marxist sculptors and members of the cooperative—exhibited their work at *PRODUGA* until the 1980s. In 1982 Demut presented her sculptural objects, inspired by memories and dream worlds, while not entirely detached from the world of ordinary objects informed by daily use. However, her fountain with a bronze stele in front of the former Restaurant Cooperativo at Werdplatz did not start its "job" until the evening before May 1, 1983.

1980S: ZURICH IN FLAMES?—FROM "SLEEPING BEAUTY" TO PUNK

At the beginning of the 1980s, then freelance curator Bice Curiger presented her own upcoming generation of artists, musicians, and impassioned amateurs at the Städtische Galerie zum Strauhof. The now undeniably trailblazing exhibition *Saus und Braus, Stadtkunst* (1980) intentionally and definitively wiped away the

---

16 Fritz Billeter, "Performance—die eigene Haut zu Markte tragen"; "Das Stadthaus segelt im Wind von 68"; "Die Produzentengalerie Zürich – wieviel Kunst darf's denn sein und welche?" in *68 Zürich steht Kopf. Rebellion, Verweigerung, Utopie*, idem and Peter Killer, eds., exh. cat., Scheidegger & Spiess, Zurich, 2008, pp. 109–127.

17 Sandi Paucic, "Hartnäckiger Kämpfer für eine neue Kunstausbildung," *Tages-Anzeiger*, Jan. 1, 2007, p. 41.

18 Gioia Dal Molin, "Kunst & Politik—die Zürcher Produzentengalerie Produga," in *1968–1978: Ein bewegtes Jahrzehnt in der Schweiz*, ed. Janick Marina Schaufelbuehl, Chronos, Zurich, 2009, pp. 271–283.

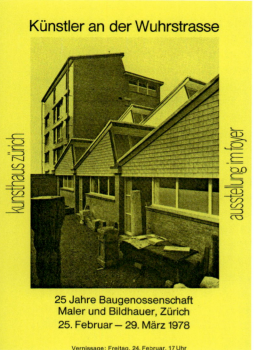

FIG. 12 Invitation for the exhibition *Künstler an der Wuhrstrasse* on the occasion of the 25th anniversary of the cooperative, Kunsthaus Zürich, 1978

boundaries between DIY and art. Curiger paired record cover design with oil paintings, pitting humor and wordplay against gravity and the lofty cultural ambitions of a postwar modernism, already perceived as philistine in the 1960s. The exhibition that Carlo Vivarelli curated to celebrate the 25th anniversary of the cooperative in the lobby of the Kunsthaus Zürich was not quite as lighthearted. (FIG. 12) Well-established Wuhrstrasse artists between thirty and forty years old contributed to the new, recently launched exhibition format. The daily press reported: "René Ed. Brauchli, [Franz] Grossert y Cañameras, Remo Roth, [Bert] Schmidmeister. In addition to sculptures, Trudi Demut is exhibiting a gray collage infused with the poetry of delicate differences; Otto Müller's Stille Tafel and Otto Teucher's stainless steel column set sculptural and personal accents. Vivarelli's colorful groupings and Hansjörg Mattmüller as the maker of a twelve-part series (Exercise de Style) demonstrate stringently constructible design. Tildy Grob-Wengér is represented by paintings and a tapestry [...], effectively contrasted with Rapport Mensch by graphic artist and painter Werner W. Wyss."[19]

Meanwhile, the Zurich band Dogbody adapted "London's Burning" by The Clash to create "Züri brännt."[20] The performance at Club Hey ended up providing the soundtrack for new activism related to the old call for an autonomous youth center (AJZ), which had been suppressed by police violence and undercover agents. During the turbulent 1980s, the Wuhrstrasse cooperative was still basically dormant, like "sleeping beauty," to use Pietro Mattioli's diplomatic euphemism. The decline in the activities of the studio cooperative at Wuhrstrasse may be attributed to a series of circumstances. For one thing, a first and second generation of members were now older and correspondingly less dynamic; secondly, the diversity of heterogeneous views and approaches had always been more cumbersome and not readily or speedily reduced to a single common denominator. Moreover, the artists residing there as members of the cooperative had no need to squat in empty buildings or to stage demonstrations that would draw attention to their need for studios and living quarters.

Klaudia Schifferle, artist and musical pioneer in the women's punk band Kleenex (1978–1984, renamed LiLiPUT in 1980), with record covers designed by Peter Fischli, was actually only a brief guest at Wuhrstrasse from 1988 to 1989. In an interview with student of art history Madleina Deplazes and art historian Dora Imhof, she speaks of the time in Zurich prior to that: "It was all new to me because I didn't come to Zurich until 1977. And then I felt the energy and excitement. The problem was that there were no places where you could settle down and celebrate. But that didn't bother me so much personally because I was always on the go anyway. For me it was like taking that energy and doing something with it. I wasn't the least bit frustrated. Naturally I thought the Rote Fabrik was great. It had just started up. We were there a lot and rehearsed there, so we experienced it in the making."[21] The Kunsthalle Zürich became an association in 1985, and a year later, in 1986, the *Aktionsraum junger Schweizer Kunst* (Action Space for Young Swiss Art, already set up at the Rote Fabrik in 1984) was officially registered as an association under the umbrella of the Shedhalle Association.[22] When the people of Zurich voted to use and subsidize the Rote Fabrik as an alternative cultural center in 1987, several studios, co-financed by the city, were included as well.

THE 1990S AND 2000S: POST-INDUSTRIAL POTENTIAL AND THE EXPANSION OF "CONTEMPORARY ART"

"More is happening in Swiss Art than ever before," as Bice Curiger summed up in the year 1998 on the occasion of her exhibition and eponymous catalog *Freie Sicht aufs Mittelmeer/Make Way for the Mediterranean* at Kunsthaus Zürich.[23] Inexpensive studios were easy to find in the abandoned, vacant industrial sites that abounded in Zurich in the 1990s. While a second wave of institutional

Press report in Archive Holdings SIK-A, Tildy Grob-Wengér artist's dossier.
Alec von Tavel, "Züri brännt," in *Hot Love: Swiss Punk & Wave, 1976–80*, ed. Lurker Grand, Edition Patrick Frey, Zurich, 2007, p. 55.

21 Klaudia Schifferle in an interview with Madleina Deplazes and Dora Imhof about "Art in Zurich in the 1980s" at the artist's studio, Rote Fabrik Zurich. Actually, Schifferle didn't have a studio at Rote Fabrik until later, between 2007 and 2017. See: https://www.oralhistoryarchiv.ch/Y/docs/interviews/Klaudia_Schifferle_30042008.pdf (accessed April 11, 2021)

22 Edith Krebs, "Kunst in Zürich," in *Kunst in der Schweiz*, eds. Pidu P. Russek, Robert Fischer, Kiepenheuer & Witsch, Cologne, 1991, pp. 139–154.
23 Bice Curiger, "Der erweiterte Horizont," in *Freie Sicht aufs Mittelmeer. Junge Schweizer Kunst mit Gästen*, exh. cat., Scalo, Zurich, 1998, p. 9.

critique was rediscovering the museum as a potential site, albeit restructured, art was also shifting to locations that could easily be transformed into an illegal techno club after nightfall. Obviously the social agenda of an "artists' colony" had not outlived its usefulness, but all the units at Wuhrstrasse were occupied while elsewhere available spaces (although temporary) were multiplying, spawning a multifarious "off scene." Furthermore, this situation may also mirror the fact that, in the course of the 1980s, the conflict over the distribution of cultural funding in Switzerland had gradually given way to an increasingly well-developed system of support from private foundations, public funds, both local and federal, as well as banks.[24]

Asked about how well versed the art scene was in Switzerland, art historian Philip Ursprung observed that "It's been nearly ten years since we dreamt away the 'quiet afternoon' while the wall came down in Berlin."[25] But by the beginning of the early 90s, the afternoons were no longer all that quiet anymore in Switzerland either, as Ursprung insinuates in his allusion to *Stiller Nachmittag/Quiet Afternoon*, an exhibition of 1987 showcasing young Swiss artists and named after a photographic piece by Fischli/Weiss.[26] In the 90s, the dialogue among the members of the cooperative at Wuhrstrasse became livelier as well and more consensus oriented. But it was only in 2003 that this self-reflection, pushed forward, among other things, thanks to Pietro Mattioli, culminated in a publication issued on the occasion of the cooperative's fifty-year anniversary, *50 Jahre Baugenossenschaft Maler und Bildhauer Wuhrstrasse 8/10*.[27]

Urs Frei is one of the protagonists of the 90s "art boom." When he moved into Wuhrstrasse 8/10 in 2001, he had already chalked up substantial artistic successes. After studying at the Staatliche Hochschule für Bildende Künste/Städelschule Frankfurt and spending some time in New York and Vienna, Frei returned to his hometown of Zurich in 1989. In 1993, at the age of thirty-five, he became the first recipient of the *Paul Valéry Anerkennungspreis für Gegenwartskunst,* a new contemporary art prize awarded by an international jury, with art theoretician and researcher Christoph Schenker as president. Frei and Helmut Federle represented Switzerland in the church of San Staë at the 1997 Venice Biennale. And in 1999, Frei added an expansive solo presentation at the Wiener Secession to his international achievements. (FIG. 13)

While the once industrial neighborhood of Zurich, pulsating with the vitality of "contemporary art" and its claim to having no history, attracted visitors from all over the world, the first decade of the new millennium also saw a proliferation of alternative art venues and off spaces, for instance, in the former working-class district of Zurich-Aussersihl. An evening would begin or end at Haus Perla-Mode (a former Jewish textile business), which artist and mediator Esther Eppstein opened up on Langstrasse for independent newcomers and their projects, including the Message Salon, the Wartesaal, the Motto Bookstore, Le Foyer, or the small gallery with which former fellow member of Les Complices* Jean-Claude Freymond-Guth had embarked on his first foray into the art market. The off-space Les Complices*, run by curator Andrea Thal from 2006 to 2016, had itself become one of the most important points of contact for the "project spaces" initiated by an upcoming generation. Thal lived at Wuhrstrasse between 2007 and 2015. In 2011, the Swiss Federal Office of Culture selected her and Thomas Hirschhorn to represent Switzerland at the Venice Biennale, where she curated a project in and around the Teatro Fundamenta Nuove.

Like Thal, Stefan Burger was also a graduate of the course in photography offered in the first decade of this century at the Zurich University of the Arts. Working as an artistic team for the first time, Thal and Burger produced a video, *Wo war Vivarelli* (2012), (FIG. 14) based on Wuhrstrasse "as a social vessel and architectural monument" and as the point of departure for their attempt "to reveal and name the layers of meaning in the building between modernist architectural tradition, the spirit of renewal, and stasis."[28]

FIG. 13   Catalog for artist Urs Frei's exhibition at Secession, Vienna, 1999

24   Patrizia Keller, *Vom Holzboden auf das internationale Kunstparkett. Die Förderung der Bildenden Kunst in der Schweiz seit 1980*, dissertation, University of Zurich, 2015.
25   Philip Ursprung, "Suisse-o-phone," in *Freie Sicht aufs Mittelmeer* (see note 23 above), p. 86.
26   *Stiller Nachmittag: Aspekte Junger Schweizer Kunst*, exh. cat., with texts by Hans Peter Ammann and Toni Stoos, Kunsthaus Zürich, Zurich, 1987.
27   Pietro Mattioli, ed., *50 Jahre Baugenossenschaft Maler und Bildhauer Wuhrstrasse 8/10*, self-published, Zurich, 2003.
28   Gabrielle Schaad in conversation with Stefan Burger, studio Wuhrstrasse 10, Zurich, Mar. 10, 2021.

FIG. 14 Andrea Thal, Stefan Burger, *Wo war Vivarelli?* HD Video, 9:22 min, 2012 (with Stefan Burger, Andreas Dobler, Urs Frei, William Lutz, Antonio Mattioli, Pietro Mattioli, Valeria Stefané-Klausmann, and Andrea Thal)

Another "generational change" has been set in motion since 2015 by Zilla Leutenegger and Veronika Spierenburg. Their cross-disciplinary approach involves a whole series of investigations into diverse social phenomena, all of which share an explicit interest in architecture, architectural forms and interiors, seeking to illuminate, transform, and come to terms with them. These investigations make a particularly strong public impact within the sphere of art-and-architecture projects, cultivated by both artists.

The extent to which built spaces in which to live and work are still a condition of artistic production has certainly been a matter of debate, sparked by the shift of artistic practice into digital and partly virtual space. Insistence on the necessity of a studio as the point of departure for artistic practice already came under fire in the 1960s and 1970s when the notion of "post-studio practice" was advanced. Subsequent widespread internationalized activities of a new, hypermobile generation of artists reinforced the sense that this physical anchor had potentially been abandoned. In the early years of the 21st century, artists enthusiastically embraced the opportunity, provided by the laptop, of creating art that is not bound to place. However, despite being perceived as uncoupled from everyday life and its physical exigencies, digital space proved to be dependent as well, inasmuch as it is defined and formed by pervasive social and political power structures. In any case, the long list of people applying to become members of the cooperative testifies to an unabated demand for the Wuhrstrasse studios and apartments as both physical and mental places to work in and socialize.

In the last few paragraphs of these fragmentary "chronicle entries," I may well have increasingly understated the cosmopolitan spirit of these former, current, international, regional, and locally active members of the cooperative at Wuhrstrasse—selected, incidentally, with no claim to being conclusive. And with reason, since the temporal spatial spheres of my current life reality are such that I probably increasingly take that cosmopolitan spirit for granted. In the meantime, the rapid growth of transversal or even trans-local networks along with and despite accelerating digitalization is actually compelling artists, critics, mediators, educators, dealers, curators, etc. to commute between different places on this planet or at least to constantly shift location. What could be more appropriate than renewed retreat to a gradually changing but nonetheless down-to-earth and enduring community—or rather a (building) cooperative?

Publication on the occasion of the 50th anniversary of
the Zurich Cooperative of Painters and Sculptors, edited
by Pietro Mattioli, self-published, 2003

MARIETA CHIRULESCU
STEPHAN JANITZKY
VERENA KATHREIN &
ARIANE MÜLLER
ADRIANA LARA
MANFRED PERNICE
CHRISTIAN PHILIPP MÜLLER
ERIK STEINBRECHER
CONSTANTIN THUN
GEORG WINTER

MARIETA CHIRULESCU
RAUM 1, 2020
INKJET PRINT ON TISSUE PAPER, 100×70 CM

STEPHAN JANITZKY
UNLESERLICHE RATSCHLÄGE AUS DEUTSCHLAND, 2020
DRAWING ON NEON PAPER, STAMPED AND ADDRESSED ENVELOPE, 29,7×21 CM EACH

VERENA KATHREIN/ARIANE MÜLLER
THEN I WOULD LIKE TO MAKE A HAPPY END FOR ONCE, 2017–2021
DRAWING (ARIANE MÜLLER) AND PHOTOGRAPHY (VERENA KATHREIN), VARIABLE DIMENSIONS

ADRIANA LARA
INVESTMENT FUNDS (FIG. 1 & 2), 2021
IN COLLABORATION WITH SAN KELLER
PHOTOGRAPHY, VARIABLE DIMENSIONS

MANFRED PERNICE
VITAX21, 2020
WSX22, 2020
BALLPOINT PEN AND INK ON PAPER, COPIED, 29,7×21 CM EACH
COURTESY GALERIE MAI 36, ZURICH

CHRISTIAN PHILIPP MÜLLER
SPAGAT, 2020
PHOTOGRAPHY, VARIABLE DIMENSIONS

ERIK STEINBRECHER
QUERFORMAT_FANTASIE, 2020
PHOTOGRAPHY, VARIABLE DIMENSIONS

CONSTANTIN THUN
*UNTITLED
(SIRIN MUNGCHAROEN, CRITERION OF CHOROGRAPHY, ALESSANDRO BAVA ARTICLE DRAWING, STRAUSBERGER PLATZDETAIL, WUHRSTRASSE 8/10)*, 2020
*UNTITLED
(ROBERT GOBER PRISON WINDOW, MOSEJ GINZBURG RHYTHM IN ARCHITECTURE, THUNTYPO, STRAUSBERGER PLATZDETAIL, WUHRSTRASSE 8/10)*, 2020
150 SHEETS OF TRANSPARENT FOIL, 29,7×21×2 CM EACH COURTESY OF THE ARTIST; SWEETWATER, BERLIN; GALLERIA FONTI, NAPLES

GEORG WINTER
ANBAU JETZT!
2021
MANIFEST

A FRIENDLY PLACE

STEFAN BURGER

The editors of this publication asked ten international figures in the field of contemporary art to react to Wuhrstrasse from a distance. They were each provided with a file containing historical and contemporary photographs and documents about Wuhrstrasse, to give them a picture of the subject to which they had been invited to respond. In dialogue with the editors, they each created a double-page spread. This rich array of material ranges from critical commentary to tender tribute.

GEORG WINTER recommends that the folkloristic architectural modernism at Wuhrstrasse be properly aired with all of its mustiness. The mold lies deep, basically ingrained in the very foundations; a determining professional practice among fine artists was incorporated into the design of the building, including the spatialization attendant upon the making of art. For Winter, the professional domestication of art practice is tantamount to an inexorably advancing atrophy that only revolution can prevent. Cultivate now! He thinks that the Wuhrstrasse residents in their studios are barking up the wrong tree. But, as we all know, that leads to the woods—and the air is obviously fresher there. So come outside and do your planting in the *terrain vague* of transition!

ARIANE MÜLLER and VERENA KATHREIN have made a contribution that refers to Burkhard Meltzer's text in this publication, linking it to their long-term shared research into being positioned in spaces. They refer to the writer's description of artists living in an age of "postmodern normalization" in the wake of modernism's normalizing aspirations. In *Diario di una femminista,*[1] Italian theorist Carla Lonzi describes her willingness, as a young producer of culture, to take all the hurdles defined by the male domain of art, eschewing everything assigned to the feminine—emotions, family ties, household, ornament, frills, gossip, fashion—in order to prevail in the male-constructed avant-garde. This is reflected in her apartment, an interior purged as much as possible of all that is personal. Architecture theorist Mark Wigley[2] argues that the white walls and cool, standardized interiors of modernism do not simply ignore personal taste in contrast to the excessively personalized interiors of the nineteenth century, but actively express the desire to escape public scrutiny by suppressing revealing personal decisions. This made it possible to fade into normativity, which was essential to the survival of marginalized groups (an issue Wigley examines primarily in terms of non-heteronormative men, whose criminalization acquired momentum with the rise of modernism). In the diametrically opposed, chaotic world outside, all that is normalized—cars, suits—takes a much more anarchistic shape with a potential for self-representation denied those in precarious positions, while others, who have nothing to fear, can certainly show chaotic interiors. (Compare photographs of men's and women's studios at Wuhrstrasse; think also of how "gay" interiors are represented in any number of TV films—standardized, tasteful rooms that invariably reflect a consciousness of being watched.)

In his *Unleserliche Ratschläge aus Deutschland* (Illegible Advice from Germany), STEPHAN JANITZKY designs an aesthetics of imploding dictatorial behavior. The recommendations indistinctly scrawled on the back of neon paper come to naught and evaporate as if written in water on a hot stone.
    The context of the subject matter is dryly pinpointed again in the choice of the stamp motif on the letters addressed to the the Painters and Sculptors Building Cooperative Zurich: Sesame Street, police, Heidi.

Often when there is talk of Wuhrstrasse, the term "realized utopia" comes into play. The opposite would probably be cloud-cuckoo-land, the city of birds in Aristophanes' play *The Birds*, which has become an idiom synonymous with ungrounded ideas.

---

[1] Carla Lonzi, *Taci, anzi parla. Diario di femminista*, Scritti di Rivolti Femininile, Milan, 1978.

[2] Mark Wigley, *White Walls, Designer Dresses: The Fashioning of Modern Architecture*, MIT Press, Cambridge, Massachusetts, 1995.

Both characteristics apply to MARIETA CHIRULESCU'S *Wolke* (Cloud). The appearance of volatile violence also resembles a worm at home in the earth and thus mediates between utopias that are in in the clouds and those that are down-to-earth.

Chirulescu's cloud also lays claim to its own utopian faculty of constantly changing and thus never being compelled to take fixed shape as art.

CHRISTIAN PHILIPP MÜLLER'S contribution serves up a curious time-space configuration, which is, of course, exactly what Wuhrstrasse is. A pastry, dubbed "Meitschibei" (cutie legs) in Swiss German, intrudes into the present like a cryptic relic of the past, like the generic masculine "Maler und Bildhauer," the painters and sculptors of the cooperative, in which the incredibly soft echo reverberates of the anabolic sculptural culture once practiced there (underpinned by the incredibly remote sound of a peening hammer).

Sculptural and painterly strategies of juxtaposition probably motivated Müller to combine the "manifold" terrycloth vase with the still yummy pastry that seems to have fallen out of time. Like the idea behind Wuhrstrasse, the vessel suggests the generosity, flexibility, and openness of being able to contain anything and everything, but it is above all a curious time-space entity.

The following are names of stock photographs:
rear-view-of-a-man-relaxing-sitting-on-a-sofa-at-home-and-looking.jpg,
man-looking-out-window-contemplating-a-future-full-of-potential.jpg,
close-up-photo-portrait-of-optimistic-thinking-imaging-his-future-guy-holding-cup-of-fresh-homemade-coffee-looking-in-window.jpg,
man-middle-aged-relaxing-moment-sofa.jpg,
home-leisure-relax-happiness-concept-man-lying-sitting-on-sofa-at-home.jpg:

Adriana Lara has culled her generic motifs from picture databases and restaged their condition of saturated coziness. A man leans back in the lounge chair, dignified and unconditionally content. The guarantee of indoor security instantly allows another man to gaze out into the distance, surmising that a future full of potential lies on the atmospherically blurred horizon.

CONSTANTIN THUN applies layers, digs them up, and mixes them with Wuhrstrasse, creating a blend of the most diverse pictures and documents, as in a notebook. Sirin Mungcharoen, an activist for democracy in Thailand, is seen gesticulating among illuminated columns. Drawings by Moisei Ginzburg on the essence of rhythm in architecture are juxtaposed with semiotic studies of movement from the Delsarte System of Oratory. The interlocked layout of human bodies in movement and the repetitive aesthetics of built rooms indicates that architecture as a source of movement and light is as much a site of formal elegance as it is an arena of social conflict and political debate. Utopias, power, utilitarian form, systems of order, hermeneutic sovereignty, and free spaces are rendered in dancing strokes or rigorous beats, while the images disappearing into the overall gray of his work indicates that, despite a feisty tenacity, everything will ultimately subside into the sediment of the Sihl River.

A subtle palette is seen in ERIK STEINBRECHER'S artful *Querformat _ Fantasie* (Landscape Format _ Fantasy). The blurred, flesh-colored plane initially suggests a body photograph. Or is it perhaps a variety of peach, after all...? The supposedly highly connotative or hackneyed term imagination (i.e., fantasy) might easily direct attention to the fantasy genre or be read as an ironic reference to kitsch. Instead, Steinbrecher summons the open, productive imagination and thereby assigns a specific location to the human brain and the perceptual apparatuses associated with it. He places a physically organized space for art in the form of an artists' cooperative side-by-side with the primordial space of artistic practice: the space of thought.

MANFRED PERNICE has drawn two vignettes of Wuhrstrasse as a friendly place. The sun is shining, while clouds get caught in the roof gables. The residents have arranged everything to suit their needs, with all potential necessities of modern life at their fingertips. They've got a helipad and a glass container, too, so it's easy to recycle their glass. There is a rooftop garden on one of the towers. The paths lead to and away from Wuhrstrasse, a place that is configured and reconfigured by its inhabitants and users as an open-ended and forever unfinished system.

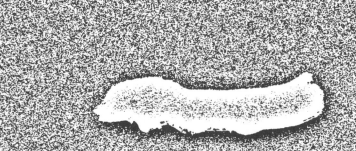

AN
BAUGENOSSENSCHAFT
MALER UND BILDHAUER ZÜRICH
WUHRSTRASSE 10
8003 ZÜRICH
SCHWEIZ

Then I would like to make a happy end for once

Casa di Carla Lonzi, (da un immagine riprodotta in
La presenza dell'uomo nel femminismo, cit.)

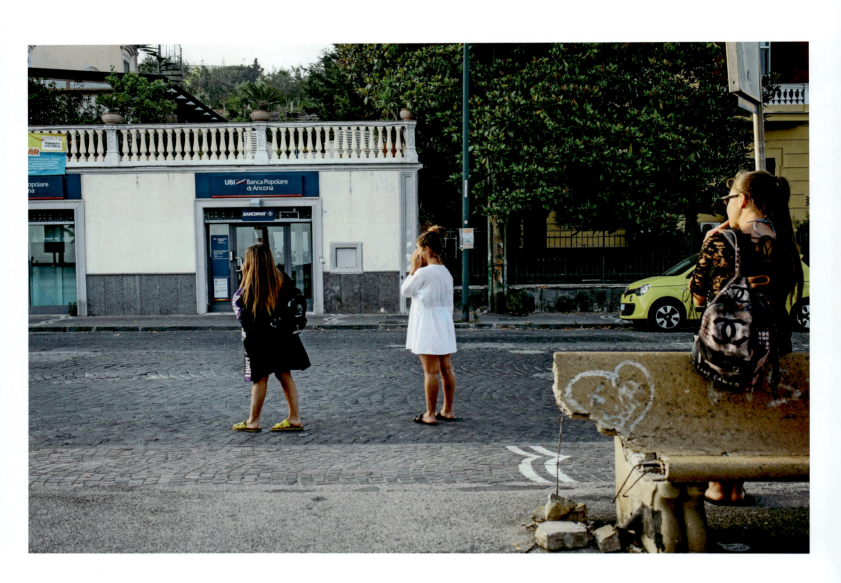

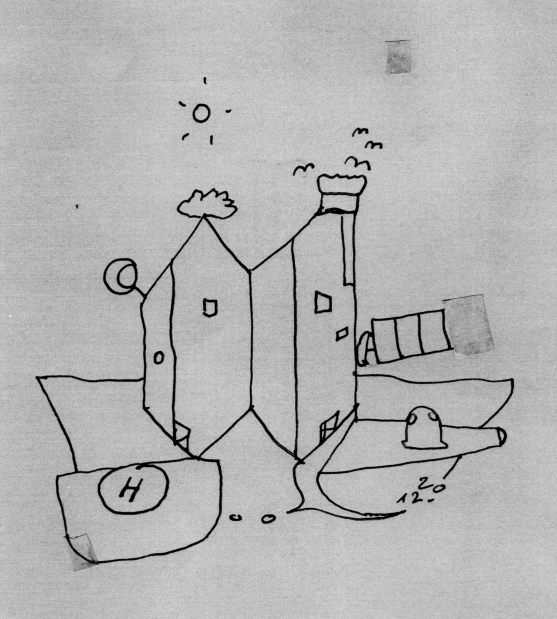

Anbau jetzt!

Wehrt euch gegen den Rückbau eures Baus!
Atelierhaus? Auf-, Ab-, und Umbau einer Genossenschaft reichen nicht aus.
Kämpft für den Anbau!
Wehrt Euch!
Erweitert den Baugrund ins freie Feld oder Beet!
Verlasst die Nebengebäude der Kunst.
Kommt ins Offene Freund*innen!*

Was tun?
Verdichtete Grundstrukturen durch neuen Grün-Dung auflockern und Sauerstoff zuführen.
Substanzielle Verdichtung, im Sinne der anastrophalen Wende, in Richtung Ertrag und Ernte, entsteht erst durch gute Durchlüftung und das Speichern von Flüssigkeiten.
Kollektive Prozesse zur Bodenlockerung, gemeinsam mit den Bodentieren, helfen, den über Jahre aufgebauten Druck zu überwinden.
Die Einengung des Wurzelwerks, kann Staunässe oder Moderprozesse verursachen, die jedoch durch Kooperationen im offenen Feld, mit Phacelia, Inkarnatklee, Gelbsenf, Studentenblume, Kapuzinerkresse, Lupine, Luzerne, Kleegras, Ölrettich, Weißer Senf, Sommer- und Winterraps u.a. verhindert werden.
Pflanzt im Terrain Vague des Übergangs!
Anbau Genoss*innen!
Gründet Anastrophal-anarchische Anbaugenossenschaften! oder künstlerische Bau- und Bäuer*innengenossenschaften!

nach Hölderlin

IN ART WE TRUST

ADAM JASPER

I am writing this text as an outsider to the *Genossenschaft* system; as an outsider, and an admirer.[1] Where marketplaces and governments have, in the past century, conclusively failed to successfully solve the housing problem, the Genossenschaft model—the term that can be loosely translated as "housing co-operative," but implies much more—has not only delivered excellent middle-class housing to low-income communities, it has also helped to politically activate them. Which is to say that, in solving the housing problem, the Genossenschaft model also addresses another perhaps even more trenchant problem: the long-term tendency to disenfranchise those social organizations that shield the individual from direct exposure to government and marketplace. This history of disintermediation is a very old one. It is arguably a driving force in the history of the city itself, from the dissolution of the guilds to the atomization of the nuclear family, and so it is perhaps not surprising that an attempt to solve the pragmatic problem of shelter should also cut to the heart of the problem of the city.

As a distant admirer (I didn't grow up in Switzerland and, unfortunately, I don't live in a Genossenschaft), there are two clusters of problems around the Genossenschaft that I do not know the answer to. Firstly, is it possible, however, to imagine the Genossenschaft model flourishing outside of the social democracies of central Europe? Can Wuhrstrasse function as a useful role model for projects outside of the special conditions of Zurich? As an outsider, it has always struck me as odd that the Swiss, who have done so much to perfect their system of government at home, have done so little to export it overseas. Unlike the British and American democratic systems that have sometimes belligerently asserted their universal applicability, the Swiss cantonal democracies, demonstrably more democratic than their Anglo-American counterparts, seem to operate on the assumption that Swiss democracy can only flourish in the shelter of the Alps. How to translate the achievement of Wuhrstrasse into a language that can leave Switzerland?

Such projects, although they are ultimately communitarian, do not spontaneously form, even (or rather, especially not) in communities where they are most desperately needed. Thus the second problem is, what are the necessary conditions for the initial formation of successful autonomous communities? Are charismatic individualists toxic to such groups, or are they rather indispensable? Is there a competition between the individual and the communal, or rather can one speak of a productive tension, and if so, what are its characteristics?

Both these questions are naive, but radical naivety is necessary in describing problems of imponderable complexity. In spite of repeated attempts to import the model by activist groups, the spread of Genossenschaften (and analogous forms like community land trusts) in Anglo-Saxon democracies, known for their turbo-charged neoliberalism, has been unsteady and slow. The self-help organizations that would enable a collective escape from the most predatory sides of the market do not seem to exist, or when they do, they take very different forms. Perhaps the perfect counterpoint is the work of Theaster Gates. Rather than tangling with political or sociological generalizations, this essay turns to a comparison between the Kolonie on the Wuhrstrasse and Theaster Gates' Rebuild Foundation. In some ways, the two scenarios couldn't be further apart. Wuhrstrasse, built in 1952 in Zurich, versus Theaster Gates' Rebuild Foundation, established half a century later in the South Side of Chicago, seem at first glance utterly disconnected. Wuhrstrasse's sober model of civic dialogue seems worlds apart from Theaster Gates' beautiful hyperbole. Nevertheless, both are paradigmatic examples of artist driven developments, and as different as they are in the methods that they employed to create solidarity and consent (if not consensus)—their ultimate aims are perhaps the same.

---

1 For this text, I rely on the following publications, among others:
Pietro Mattioli (ed.), *50 Jahre Baugenossenschaft Maler und Bildhauer Wuhrstrasse 8/10*, Eigenverlag, Zürich 2003.
Carol Becker and Achim Borchardt-Hume, *Theaster Gates*, Phaidon Press, London 2015.

John Colapinto, "The Real Estate Artist", in: *The New Yorker*, Vol. 89, No 45, 20.1.2014.
Tom McDonough, "Theaster Gates," in: *Bomb*, Issue 130, 2015.
Theaster Gates, *12 Ballads for Huguenot House*, Walther Koenig, Chicago 2012.

But back to the beginning: In Zurich, in the wake of the destruction of World War II, three impoverished artists set out to persuade the city to enable them to build an institution—two sculptors, both named Otto—Otto Müller and Otto Teucher—and a painter called Max Truninger. At the time, artists were viewed as undesirable as neighbors. Their lives were held to be fraught with instability, their livers ruined by alcohol, and so on. Consequently, they were largely shut out of the projects for affordable housing that Genossenschaften had established in the city of Zurich over the previous decades, in the years after the First World War and during the Great Depression.

The three artists, under the encouragement of a young architect, Ernst Gisel, set out to change this perception. In such a campaign, there is, and must be, a dance with power, or perhaps even more directly, a small conspiracy. In the case of the Wuhrstrasse artists, from the very beginning they were under the spell of Ernst Gisel, who was close to his old teacher Alfred Roth. Roth, in turn, was close to the city president, Emil Landolt, and the editor of the most influential architecture magazine, *Werk* (such magazines mattered more in the 1940s, in the years in which reconstruction was the project of all of Europe, than they matter now). Theaster Gates, for his part, had the support of the mayor of Chicago, Rahm Emanuel, and beyond him, Barack Obama (whose own house is allegedly a couple of miles away), but we will return to him later.

Roth published Gisel's initial plans for a settlement for painters and sculptors in an article in 1948 as an "ideal project." Gisel, who had been close to the arts and enthusiastic about the concept of the Genossenschaft, was the untiring agitator behind the scenes. He was not yet thirty years old. The state did not sell the colony the land, but permitted them the right to build upon it and provided an interest-free mortgage for the building. The state, so to speak, helped by getting out of the way. As an aside, this offers us a working definition of utopia: utopia is a piece of muddy land without rules, without traditions, and without restrictions.

The emphasis in the first *Werk* announcement was on the functional intelligence of the architecture: the sculptors would be on the ground floor. The painters upstairs. Studios would exist directly under the roof. But the architectural intelligence was secondary to the project's success. Whether the design was good or bad is almost irrelevant; rather in its details, it had to achieve two things: to give the political project an air of physical reality, a sense that it is concrete and plausible. Secondly, to give the impression that the building was only suited to a single function: that once it was built, it couldn't be appropriated for other purposes. As a building designed to allow artists to be productive, it could in turn produce only artists. Customized functionalism, here, is a kind of bureaucratic finger trap, a means to prevent the site from being reabsorbed into the general housing stock of the city. The effect of this design maneuver, the attempt to make the building look both residential and industrial, was to create a building that anticipated later architectural tastes. From the street, it presents itself as a modest, red-brick walk-up, one that, from a distance, could be mistaken for a residential building from the 1970s, except for the skillion roof, which hinted at its second role as a light industrial building. On the façade, a bronze relief featuring a four-legged avatar of the building by Otto Müller was the sole overt ornament, but it hinted at the symbolic importance of the house.

In 1955, some years later, the magazine *Werk* revisited the project. Instead of being based on drawings, it was based on photography. Where the drawings conveyed the earnestness of Ernst's conception, the photographs established the success of the built project through the multiplicity of small, visible proofs of life and hospitality in the studio, through articles of clothing draped casually on furniture or cups on surfaces. In multiple photographs, a large black cat appears, as a kind of studio-familiar, to show that this is a place both of work and repose.

Part of the genius of Wuhrstrasse was the absence of a binding vision—the Wuhrstrasse group was not about forming a school, or a style of art. There was no manifesto about the content of art that was capable of falling out of favor. The architecture did not even insist on communal living. The artists were permitted, through the luxury of space, to become middle class, to become boring. The absence of an agenda helped the colony to endure. The intelligence of this absence of vision becomes even clearer when considering that one of the current limitations of the community is the division of spaces into dedicated slots for sculptors and painters, genre distinctions that are no longer crucial to the arts, but that in the 1950s seemed eternal.

By the mid-1950s, Wuhrstrasse had become glamorous, in a small-scale, Zurich way. Popular illustrated magazines visited it to photograph the bohemian yet cozy lives of local artists. Photos were shot from angles that evoked the mansard roofs of Paris, but the images spoke as much of cake and tea as of radical art. For nearly 70 years—that is to say, a time span that covers multiple generations—Wuhrstrasse has thrived. At what point does a community group become an institution? The triumph of Wuhrstrasse is that it became uncontroversial, even to its neighbors. Invisibility equals success, because it requires stability. The tragedy of Wuhrstrasse is that it allowed artists to join the middle classes, but did not reciprocally transform the middle classes into artists. But this is no tragedy at all.

Theaster Gates cannot afford to not be controversial. He works in an environment in which provocation is necessary for publicity, and visibility is necessary for survival. Take his "Artist Strategy for 21st Century Engagement" in which he asserts six rules:

1. Assume nothing can be perfect.
2. Everything you do will be perceived as gentrification.
3. Don't forget parking + storage.
4. Creativity requires understanding of pre-existing systems and willingness to craft new ones.
5. Disseminating ideas is easy for corporations and large institutions—tending to the needs of communities requires more vigilance/intention/clarity of thought + execution.
6. Only God saves. We got tactics.

Theaster Gates is an unusual figure. As a young black student, he went to an elite school in Chicago, and thereafter spent a year in Tokoname, Japan, studying pottery. He straddled all the categories that might have defined him, or trapped him. For a decade after, he worked for the Chicago Transport Authority, developing public art projects.

In 2008, in the wake of the subprime mortgage bust, the clapboard bungalow next to Gates's South Side home went on the market for $16,000. Inspired by Rick Lowe's *Project Row Houses* (1993, ongoing—Lowe was in turn inspired by Joseph Beuys), Gates bought it, gutted it, and filled it with the book collection of John H. Johnson, founder of *Ebony* and *Jet* magazines, and slides of the collections of the University of Chicago and the Art Institute of Chicago. He called it *Archive House*. He used the scrap material from properties to make shoeshine stands (tokens of the sub-proletarian labor that Blacks used to perform in the city) that he in turn sold for thousands at Miami Art Basel. With the proceeds, he bought another house. The ex-candy store where he lived, he converted into a store for the record collection of Frankie Knuckles, the godfather of house music, and renamed it *Listening House*. At the 2012 *documenta* in Kassel, Theaster Gates squatted and restructured Hugenot House, constructing furniture out of the remnants of both buildings from Dorchester Avenue, and remains he found in the ruined interior. The improvised furniture was later sold as art. In 2013, with the proceeds, Theaster Gates bought an abandoned bank, the Stony Island State Savings Bank, from the City of Chicago. The bank, now known as the *Stony Island Arts Bank*, was due to be demolished. Gates had to personally persuade the Chicago mayor Rahm Emmanuel to intervene to stop the demolition. The monumental pediment and classical columns of the bank's façade was, as Gates pointed out, a source of pride for the community. Style and ideology have a complicated relationship.

Dorchester Avenue on the South Side of Chicago, where the Stony Island State Savings Bank stood dilapidated, is one of the poorest neighborhoods in the city. Nineteen out of twenty of the residents are Black. At the same time, the visual effects of poverty are not what you see in Hollywood films. Although many properties are boarded up, there is relatively little graffiti, and the streets are empty. Abandoned houses are demolished by the city to discourage crime, and in neighborhoods like this, they are demolished in their hundreds. The ravages of decline are marked not by dense slums, but rather, by a kind of re-ruralization. Between modest, carefully maintained brownstones are ever-expanding fields of grass.

FIG. 1 Theater Gates, *Dorchester Art Housing Collaborative,* Chicago

FIG. 2 Share No. 001 of the Zurich Cooperative of Painters and Sculptors, October 1, 1952

FIG. 3 Theater Gates, *Bank Bond*, 2013, Marble, 15.5 × 21.9 × 2.1 cm

What Gates did was mimic the power structures around him. Instead of setting up a Genossenschaft (who would know what that was, on the South Side?) he posed initially as a developer. By 2017 he had accumulated some 32 properties and employed scores of people (the activities of his organizations are published annually in a format that both mocks and perfectly emulates a corporate financial report). Part of the genius of Gates's approach is that he does not fight gentrification, but embraces it. He openly claims he wishes to see gentrification of Black neighborhoods, but by Black citizens. As evidence for his success, he organized a group of public policy students from the Harris School of the University of Chicago to assess the impact of his work on the South Side neighborhood of Washington Park, and they determined that a rise in housing value around his institutions, and a concurrent decline in the average proportion of income paid in rent, indicated an ongoing economic enrichment of the neighborhood that is geographically at the center of an area of increasing poverty.

At the same time as this model seems completely distinct to that of the Genossenschaft, at certain moments the overlap is almost perfect. As Exhibit A, take this reproduction of an *Anteilschein*, or share certificate. The first one issued was issued in October 1952 to the painter Walter Haymann for the sum of 100 Swiss Francs. Haymann never lived in the Genossenschaft, but his purchase of a certificate helped to raise the funds required for the project. Likewise, the Stony Island Arts Bank, the first of Theater Gates's projects, also issued 100 share certificates. Except that his were engraved on marble taken from the urinals of the derelict South Chicago Bank, and he sold them not to members, but to collectors at Art Basel for $5,000 each. On those tablets was engraved "In Art We Trust."

The Dorchester Art + Housing Cooperative, also known as Dante Harper, after the avenues that neighbor the site, was originally designed by the Chicago Housing Authority as low-income community housing in the 1970s, and opened in 1981 with thirty-six units in two-story structures. It followed what at the time were the orthodoxies of public housing. Since the publication of Oscar Newman's urban planning classic, *Defensible Space*, a book whose publication coincided with the destruction of the Pruitt-Igoe housing development in St. Louis, public housing had been low rise and modest. It had been built in red brick with large windows—which is to say, in materials and proportions strikingly similar to the Wuhrstrasse Genossenschaft—by what in the US was already referred to as a "minority contractor"—a Black-owned construction business. The homes were well built, but by 2011, when discussions began, they had been abandoned for four years, victims of the slow depopulation of the neighborhood. When Rebuild, Gates's foundation, took control of the site, together with Landon Bone Baker architects, it included not only their renovation and landscaping, but also converted four units into a shared arts center. Now, Dorchester Art + Housing Cooperative offers housing to artists, who—and this is the twist—must pass a selection committee consisting of people living in the local community. In 2016, the project won an AIA/HUD award. Since then, the absence of controversial news about Dante Harper in the press can be taken as an indication of success: it is doing what it was intended to do, providing shelter.

At the center of Gates's practice (he uses the list as a form of manifesto) are what he calls the "7 Principles of Ethical Redevelopment":

1. Repurpose and re-propose: Take stock of what is around you.
2. Engaged Participation: Invite others to get involved.
3. Pedagogical Moments: Moments of learning and teaching unfold in all aspects of work.
4. The indeterminate: Suspend knowing.
5. Design: Beauty is a basic service.
6. A sense of place cannot be developed overnight.
7. Stack, leverage, and access: Scale

Gates's manifestos are ultimately about agency. He has the drive, and charisma, of an entrepreneur, although his motivation is communitarian. In his world view, the levers of the capitalist machine should not be left only to the capitalists. It is also to be noted that his enthusiasm for ownership is also a question of security. It is a privilege of social democracies that membership in a Genossenschaft is security enough to ensure continuity of housing. In Chicago—let alone third-world economies—economic shocks are frequent enough, and severe enough, that collective ownership remains for most a provisional arrangement, something that might suit artist's residencies, but is not secure enough for families, who desperately wish to own their homes. This realization also influenced Gates's approach to the refurbishment of city-owned, low-income housing.

One of the ironies behind the entire enterprise is that Gates is an aesthete. He speaks only of politics, but his taste, honed on the meticulous study of Japanese pottery, is astonishingly refined. His work is so beautiful that it would be inadmissible to contemporary art circles, if it was not that he had the alibi of accessibility and community activism with which to excuse its beauty. His love of patina, weathered timbers, tar paintings, and respect for artisanal skills is so untimely that it requires a political justification.

The generations of the two projects are different, and the context is different. In Zurich, context is everything: projects, to be credible, need to appear to emerge organically from the needs and traditions of the city. In Chicago, context is both contingent and a source of possibility. It's an obstacle that you can turn into an opportunity.

To what extent can we claim that there is a family relationship between Wuhrstrasse and the Dorchester Art+Housing Cooperative, these two red-brick shelters for artists on opposite sides of the Atlantic? Is the resemblance between the two institutions deceptive, because the legal and economic regimes that gave rise to them are so dissimilar, or because they inhabit such different cities? In both cases, there is something of the Protestant revolution latent in the language of the movements (Zwinglist on one side, and Baptist on the other). There is a refusal of charity: the artist's wish for studios and affordable living spaces, not as alms from the wealthy of the city, but in order to be able to work. They struggle for autonomy, and for self-sufficiency, but it is not a demand, in the sense of a request, because there is no higher power that can award such self-sufficiency.

Or is there a common shared denominator in the genesis of the two projects, in the charismatic figures that generated them, in the case of Zurich, the tireless Ernst Gisel, who agitated unceasingly to realize his projects in collaboration with Otto Müller, Otto Teucher, and Max Truninger, and in the case of Chicago, Theaster Gates, who transformed himself into a showman in order to realize his? Is individual charisma necessary for such projects, that by their nature are exceptions to the regular calculus of profit and loss used by developers, and for that reason, potentially all the more profitable?

This text is a plea addressed to readers who can study their role models, and choose their utopias, as both Gates and Ernst have done—not only to solve questions, but to *make* something. It is not that the enemy is at the levers of capitalism, so much as that there is no one at the levers at all. There is also a craft in making out of the invisible web of legal constraints, economic interests, and historical failures a net of possibilities to catch an as yet unrealized world.

BIOGRAPHIES

Georg Aerni is an artist and a photographer; he lives and works in Zürich. After studying architecture and working in that field for several years, Aerni taught himself photography in the 1990s. In addition to commissioned work in architectural photography, he has since devoted himself to the artistic study of our built and natural environment, particularly large cities and cultural landscapes. He has published several books of photography with Scheidegger & Spiess and in 2011 he was received the German Photo Book Award in Silber for his monograph *Sites & Signs*. In his photographic series, Aerni does not seek out global common ground but instead focuses on local aspects. He reads respective settings—even when deserted—as sign spaces that say something about history as well as social and cultural living conditions.

Stefan Burger is a photographer and an artist. He studied photography at the Zurich University of the Arts (ZHdK, 1999–2003), lives and works in Zurich, and has been living at the Painters and Sculptors Building Cooperative Zurich since 2010. He worked with the chair of architecture and art Prof. Karin Sander at the ETH Zürich (2012–2015). In 2012 he won the Follow Fluxus grant awarded by the Kunstverein Wiesbaden and was a fellow at the Istituto Svizzero in Rome (2015/16). His works have been on view in solo exhibitions at Galerie Kirchgasse, Steckborn (2020), Kunsthalle Bern (2017), Fotomuseum Winterthur (2010), and Kunstmuseum Stuttgart (2009). Burger curated the double-page art inserts in this publication, in which widely diverse artistic strategies are interwoven with the realities of Wuhrstrasse.

Marieta Chirulescu is an artist, who lives and works in Berlin. She studied painting at the Hochschule für Bildenden Künste Nürnberg (1998–2004) and at the Hungarian Academy of the Fine Arts in Budapest. Chirulescu has presented solo exhibitions at Foksal Gallery Foundation, Warsaw (2019), Kurimanzutto, Mexico City (2016), White Cube Bermondsey, London (2011), and Kunsthalle Basel (2010). She has also contributed to group exhibitions, including *#12 / Folies d'hiver*, Villa Medici, Rome (2017), *Image Support*, Kunsthalle Bergen (2014), *Nur was nicht ist möglich*, Museum Folkwang, Essen, (2013), *Space, Space*, Museum Vasarely, Budapest, (2014), and *Minimal Myth*, Museum Boijmans Van Beuningen, Rotterdam (2012).

Stephan Janitzky is an artist. He works in Munich at the Academy of Fine Arts. He is coeditor of the artists' journal *muss sterben* with Sebastian Stein. musssterben.org

Adam Jasper is the editor of *gta papers* and contributes regularly to such magazines as *Cabinet Magazine* and *Artforum*. In 2019, he curated the installation *Priests and Programmers* at the Sharjah Architecture Triennial. Adam Jasper took his doctorate in art history at the Power Institute of the University of Sydney.

Verena Kathrein is a photographer and lives in Munich. She does commissioned work, portraits and landscape photography, as well as working on her own photography within the art context. Ariane Müller is an artist and writer and lives in Berlin. She teaches at the Umeå Academy of Fine Arts, is coeditor of *Starship Magazine* and worked for many years as a political consultant for UN-HABITAT in Nairobi. Kathrein and Müller worked together on the research for *Then I would like to make a happy end for once,* which has been on view in various formats, for instance at Museion Bozen, Kunstverein Nürnberg, and Starship in Berlin. In their shared commentary on Wuhrstrasse, they view the apartment and studio building as a form of political private space.

Caroline Kesser is an art historian, art critic, curator, and writer of numerous essays. She lives in Zurich. As a member of the art committee of the City of Zurich and through her work for the art collection of the City of Zurich, she is extremely well-versed in the history of art in Zurich. Her book of Augusto Giacometti's previously unpublished diaries from the years 1932–1937, *Immer nur das Paradies*, was published in 2020 by Verlag Scheidegger & Spiess.

Adriana Lara is an artist and lives in Mexico City. Her projects investigate the connections between structure, style, content, and form in order to redefine value and meaning in cultural production. Her work transposes systems of order into formal, abstract sign systems, in order to illuminate the mechanics of status that are so dominant in today's world. Her work has been presented in solo exhibitions, in such venues as Midway Contemporary Art, Minneapolis (2018), Greenspon Gallery, New York (2017), and Galerie Air de Paris, Paris (2015). Group exhibitions include Kunstverein Bielefield, Galerie OMR, Mexico City (2019), the Swiss Institute, New York (2018), Pérez Art Museum, Miami (2017), Nouveau Musée National de Monaco (2017), and SculptureCenter, New York (2016). In 2012, Lara was represented at *documenta 13* in Kassel.

Pietro Mattioli is an artist. He has been living at the Painters and Sculptors Building Cooperative Zurich on Wuhrstrasse since 1993. After taking the preliminary course at the Zurich School of Applied Art (1974/75), he trained as a photographer with H.J. Henn in Zurich (1975–1978). Lived in London (1990–1992). Worked at Fotomuseum in Winterthur (1994–2008). He was a curator at the CoalMine Fotogalerie in Winterthur, specializing in contemporary Swiss photography (2003–2006), lecturer at the F+F School of Art and Design (2005–2012), member of the art committee of the City of Zurich (2006–2014), and a member of the AG KiöR [art in public space] of the City of Zurich (2006–2009). He has presided over the Painters and Sculptors Building Cooperative Zurich since 2002.

Bruno Maurer studied art at the University of Zurich. He was an assistant at the Faculty of Art and Architectural History at ETH Zürich (1988–1993) and editor of the journal *archithese* (1992–1995). Since 1994, he has been responsible for coordinating research at the Institute of the History and Theory of Architecture (gta) of the ETH Zürich. In 2001, he additionally became head of the gta archives. He has created numerous exhibitions as well as publishing widely, including monographs as well as catalogs and newspaper articles primarily on the history of architecture in the nineteenth and twentieth centuries. Together with Werner Oechslin he is the editor of *Ernst Gisel Architekt* (gta Verlag 1993, revised 2010).

Burkhard Meltzer is a writer, lecturer, and curator. He lives in Zurich. After studying photography in Dortmund and Zurich, he joined the curatorial team at Kunsthalle St. Gallen (2003–2007). Since 2007, he has worked as a freelance curator, mounting such projects as *Gibst Du mir Steine, geb ich Dir Sand* (2012), *Rethinking the Modular* (2015), and *A Chair, projected* (2019). He has contributed to such magazines as a*rtforum.com, form, frieze* and also to books on contemporary art, architecture, and design. Recent publications, as coeditor, include *It's not a Garden Table—Kunst und Design im erweiterten Feld* (JRP-Ringier, 2011), *Ausstellen—Zur Kritik der Wirksamkeit in den Künsten* (Diaphanes, 2016), and *Rethinking the Modular* (Thames & Hudson, 2016). From 2012–2014, Meltzer studied literature, art, and media sciences at the University of Constance and took his doctor's degree in the history of art and design at the University of Wuppertal in 2019. Kulturverlag Kadmos, Berlin, published his thesis as a monograph in 2020: *Das ausgestellte Leben—Design in Kunstdiskursen nach den Avantgarden.* Since 2006, Meltzer has also been active as a visiting lecturer and researcher, for instance, at the Zurich University of the Arts (ZHdK).

Christian Philipp Müller studied experimental design at the F+F Schule in Zurich (1982–1984), and subsequently with Fritz Schwegler and Kasper König at the Kunstakademie Düsseldorf. He lived in Brussels (1988–1992) and New York City (1992–2011). He has been based in Berlin since 2011. He has had solo exhibitions, among others, at the Palais des Beaux-Arts in Brussels and the Kunstverein in Munich and has been represented in numerous international exhibitions. In 1993, he represented Austria at the Venice Biennale along with Andrea Fraser and Gerwald Rockenschaub. Contributed to *documenta X* (2007) and *documenta 13* (2012). In 2011, Müller was appointed professor of performative sculpture at the Kunsthochschule Kassel and was also dean. In 2016, he was awarded the Prix Meret Oppenheim.

Manfred Pernice is an artist. He lives and works in Berlin. He studied graphic arts and painting at the Hochschule für Bildenden Künste in Braunschweig (1984–1987) and sculpture at the Hochschule der Künste in Berlin (1988–1993). After having a chair at the Akademie der bildenden Künste in Vienna (2004–2009), he was appointed professor of sculpture at the Universität der Künste in Berlin in 2013. Pernice was represented at the Venice Biennale in 2001 and 2003 and at *documenta XI* Kassel in 2002, participated in the *São Paulo Biennial* (2011), *Skulptur Projekte Münster* (2007), Art Biennial of Seville (2006), *Manifesta 3* in Ljubljana (2000), the *Berlin Biennale* (1998), and the Biennale of Lyon (1997).

Zara Pfeifer is a photographer and artist. She lives and works in both Vienna and Berlin. She studied architecture at the TU Wien (BA) and at the Academy of Fine Arts (MA), followed by studies in photography at the Friedl Kubelka, all in Vienna. Zara Pfeifer is also a lecturer in architecture at the TU Wien. Her work reflects her interest in social and spatial phenomena, from the social life of the modernist housing project *Alterlaa* to sitting in the passenger seat of an 18 wheeler en route through Europe. In her long-term projects, Pfeifer becomes involved in the world she is documenting not as an observer but as an active participant. She explores places and issues not only by using photography as a tool of artistic research; she also communicates in the form of films, mappings, and lectures.

Garielle Schaad is a postdoc at the chair of Theory and History of Architecture, Art, and Design at TU Munich and research assistant Zurich University of the Arts (ZHdK). She studied the history of art and architecture at the University of Zurich, at the EPHE/Sorbonne in Paris, and Sophia University in Tokyo, and took a doctor's degree at ETH Zurich. Her research specialties include concepts of space and volume in transcultural art and design since the 1960s as well as spatialization of power and gender. She has written numerous papers on the way in which the critical, spatial practices of art and architecture overlap. She is coeditor of *archithese reader: Critical Positions in Search of Postmodernity, 1971–1976* (Zurich: Triest, 2021) and author of a monograph on the Japanese artist Shizuko Yoshikawa (Zurich: Lars Müller Publishers, 2018).

Erik Steinbrecher is an artist. He lives and works in Berlin. His work includes sculpture, photography, prints, and especially artists' books. He taught at Zurich University of the Arts (ZHdK), 2008–2020.

Constantin Thun is an artist. He lives and works in Berlin. He has had solo exhibitions at Sweetwater, Berlin; Youth Club, London; and Galleria Fonti, Naples; and in 2021 at Galleria Fonti, Naples and Galeriea Galerie: A, Bern. Contributions to group exhibitions include Mavra, Paros; Point Centre for Contemporary Art, Nicosia; Der TANK, Basel; Astrup Fearnley Museum, Oslo; and Elaine, Museum für Gegenwartskunst, Basel.

Georg Winter is an artist, based in Saarbrücken, Stuttgart, and Budapest. Characteristic of artistic practice are temporary laboratories, urban situations, self-organizing performances, and research projects in an interdisciplinary context. Since the introduction in the 1980s of his *Ukiyo Camera Systems*, the artist ranks among the activists of expanded media and space-oriented experimental art. Ambulant teaching, professorships, and revolts alternate with exercises in differentiating objects, sleep accompaniment, and the administration of sedatives to "architoxic" locations. He has been underway since 1994 with his *University in a Suitcase*, for instance, at University of Stuttgart, the Merz Academy—University of Design, Art, and Media, Stuttgart, and the Zurich University of the Arts (ZHdK, 1999–2003). He was a professor of art and public space at the Academy of Fine Arts in Nuremberg (2003–2007) and, since 2007, he has been a professor of sculpture/public art at the University of the Fine Arts in Saar.

Stefan Zweifel is a writer. When he was 17 he started translating Marquis de Sade's monumental two-volume novel *Justine und Juliette* from French to German. He writes for the *Neue Zürcher Zeitung,* the *Tages-Anzeiger,* the journals *du* and *Literaturen,* and for the literary sections of several German newspapers as well. In addition, he has taken the lead in exhibitions on dada and Surrealism, most recently curating the exhibition *Dada Universal* (2016) with Juri Steiner as a continuation of the exhibition *1900–1914: Expedition ins Glück* (2014), both at the Swiss National Museum in Zurich. He participated in Swiss television's *Literaturclub* (2007–2014). In 2009, Zweifel launched *Reflektorium* at the Burgtheater in Vienna, a series of conversations with art practitioners and intellectuals which he has since continued as *Zweifels Zwiegespräche* at Schauspielhaus Zürich. Since 2016, he has embarked on literary journeys of discovery at Miller's Studio in his series *Literatur Hoch Zwei*.

IMAGE CREDITS

Despite best efforts, we have not been able to identify the holders of copyright and printing rights for all the illustrations. Copyright holders not mentioned in the credits are asked to substantiate their claims, and recompense will be made according to standard practice.

Aargauer Kunsthaus Aarau, Inv. No. 3609: p. 193, fig. 9
Aargauer Kunsthaus Aarau/acquired with a contribution from the
    Nationalbank, Inv. No. 3967: p. 193, fig. 9
Archiv Baugenossenschaft Maler und Bildhauer Zürich: pp. 34/35, fig. 14;
    pp. 36/37, fig. 15; p. 38, fig. 20, 21; pp. 53–55, pp. 60–63, p. 91,
    pp. 98/99, p. 103, p. 119, p. 135, p. 158, fig. 4; p. 162, p. 168,
    pp. 170/171, p. 173, p. 188, p. 191, fig. 1, 3; p. 192, fig. 5, 6, 7;
    p. 195, fig. 12; p. 197, fig. 14; p. 199, p. 233, fig. 2
Archiv Baugenossenschaft Maler und Bildhauer Zürich, Tildy Grob-Wengér
    Estate: p. 50
Photographer unknown; Archiv Baugenossenschaft Maler und Bildhauer
    Zürich: p. 72, p. 92, p. 93 below, p. 158, fig. 1, 2; p. 159, fig. 2; p. 163
Photographer unknown; Pietro Mattioli's archive, Silvio Mattioli Estate:
    p. 110, fig. 1–4; p. 111, p. 116, fig. 3
Iwan Schumacher; Doris Stauffer's archive, Graphische Sammlung der
    Schweizerischen Nationalbibliothek Bern: p. 194, fig. 10
Max Hellstern; Baugeschichtliches Archiv der Stadt Zürich (BAZ):
    p. 32, fig. 7, 8, 9; p. 33, fig. 11
Photographer unknown; Baugeschichtliches Archiv der Stadt Zürich (BAZ):
    p. 33, fig. 12, 16
Photographer unknown Baugeschichtliches Archiv der Stadt Zürich (BAZ),
    Tildy Grob-Wengér Estate: p. 192, fig. 4
Walter Läubli; copyright Walter Läubli/Fotostiftung Schweiz: p. 131
Hugo P. Herdeg and Walter Binder; gta Archiv/ETH Zürich, Ernst Gisel
    Estate; Baugeschichtliches Archiv der Stadt Zürich (BAZ): pp. 21–28
gta Archiv/ETH Zürich, Ernst Gisel Estate: p. 30, fig. 3; p. 31, fig. 5;
    p. 39, fig. 17; pp. 44–49, pp. 64–71
Photographer unknown; gta Archiv/ETH Zürich, Ernst Gisel Estate:
    p. 51, p. 52, pp. 56–59
Photographer unknown; gta Archiv/ETH Zürich, Haefeli Moser Steiger:
    p. 38, fig. 19
Walter Binder; gta Archiv/ETH Zürich, Nachlass Ernst Gisel: p. 38, fig. 18
Hans Finsler; gta Archiv/ETH Zürich, Ernst Gisel Estate; Hans Finsler
    Estate, Kulturstiftung Sachsen-Anhalt, Kunstmuseum Moritzburg
    Halle (Saale): p. 89, p. 90 above
Hugo P. Herdeg; gta Archiv/ETH Zürich, Ernst Gisel Estate: p. 30, fig. 1;
    p. 42, p. 43
Ralph Hut; gta Archiv/ETH Zürich, Ernst Gisel Estate: p. 31, fig. 4
Fritz Maurer; gta Archiv/ETH Zürich, Nachlass Ernst Gisel: p. 40, fig. 23
Willy Walter; gta Archiv/ETH Zürich, Willy Walter Estate: p. 95
Hermann Winkler; gta Archiv/ETH Zürich, Ernst Gisel Estate: p. 30, fig. 2;
    Copyright F.L.C.; 2021 Pro Litteris, Zurich: p. 40, fig. 22
Leo Gantenbein; 2021 Pro Litteris, Zurich: p. 164, fig. 2
Eliette McCouch; SIK-ISEA, Zurich, Schweizerisches Kunstarchiv: p. 94
Photographer unknown; SIK-ISEA, Zurich, Schweizerisches Kunstarchiv:
    p. 105, p. 108, p. 193, fig. 8
Roland Gretler; SIK-ISEA, Zurich, Schweizerisches Kunstarchiv: p. 194, fig. 11
Photographer unknown; Stiftung Trudi Demut und Otto Müller: p. 107, p. 112,
    p. 116, fig. 1; p. 124, fig. 1, 2, 3, p. 125
Serge Stauffer; Zurich University of the Arts (ZHdK)/Archive: p. 90 below
Paul Scherrer, semester project Fotoreportage über Frau Wengér-Grob
    (1958); Zurich University of the Arts (ZHdK)/Archive: p. 93 below
Photographer unknown; Hugo Stüdeli, Otto Morach Estate: p. 117, fig. 2, 3,
    p. 120
Private collection, Switzerland: p. 31, fig. 6
Silvio R. Baviera: p. 159, fig. 3
Monika Bischof: p. 165, fig. 1, 3
Hannes R. Bossert; Hannes R. Bossert Estate: pp. 128/129
Barbara Davatz: p. 165, fig. 2
Walter Dräyer: p. 117, fig. 1; p. 164, fig. 1
Urs Frei; Secession Wien: p. 196, fig. 13
Courtesy © Theaster Gates. Image: White Cube, photographer: Ben Westoby:
    p. 233, fig. 3
H.R. Giger; copyright HR Giger Estate: p. 156, p. 157
Aldo Jotti: p. 104, fig. 3
Fred E. Knecht; Mona Knecht, Fred E. Knecht Estate: p. 104, fig. 4; p. 116, fig. 2
Pietro Mattioli: p. 33, fig. 13; p. 165, fig. 4
Zach Mortice; Rebuild Foundation Chicago: p. 233, fig. 1
Peter Münger: p. 32, fig. 10; p. 167
Jean-Luc Nicollier: S. 191, fig. 2
Michael Speich; Sabina Speich, Michael Speich Estate: p. 100, p. 240
Willy Spiller: p. 132, p. 158, fig. 3; p. 159, fig. 1; p. 164, fig. 3
Kurt Staub: p. 104, fig. 1, 2
Martin Stollenwerk; Lena Schliep, Karl Hebeisen Estate: p. 115

Art Inserts
Georg Aerni: pp. 174–187
Zara Pfeifer: pp. 3–16, pp. 73–88, pp. 137–152, pp. 244–260
Marieta Chirulescu: pp. 208/209
Stephan Janitzky: pp. 210/211
Verena Kathrein/Ariane Müller: pp. 212–215
Adriana Lara: pp. 216/217
Manfred Pernice: pp. 218/219
Christian Philipp Müller: pp. 220/221
Erik Steinbrecher: pp. 222/223
Constantin Thun: pp. 224/225
Georg Winter: pp. 226/227

Wood column, sculpture by Silvio Mattioli in the courtyard workshop, autumn 1953

ACKNOWL-EDGMENTS

The publication of this book was supported by

Amt für Hochbauten Stadt Zürich
Cassinelli-Vogel Stiftung
Else von Sick Stiftung
Ernst Göhner Stiftung
Ernst & Olga Gubler-Hablützel Stiftung
Eternit Niederurnen
Finanzdepartement Stadt Zürich
Fachstelle Kultur Kanton Zürich
Kresau 4-Stiftung

Ernst Gisel
Margrit Keiser Gisel Läubli
Pierre and Lilly Levis

Dedicated in deep gratitude to Ernst Gisel (1922–2021) in whose inspiring rooms the artists of the Painters and Sculptors Building Cooperative Zurich have been able to work and live since 1953.

Special thanks go to Maja Aeschbacher, Marina Albisini, Ian Anüll, Luigi Archetti, Ralph Bänziger, Franz Bartel, Silvio Baviera, Roger Boltshauser, Anton Bruhin, Sabine Class, Barbara Davatz, Mirjam Fischer, Fischli/Weiss, Dora Frey, Elisabeth Garzoli, Bob Gramsma, Christian Herdeg, Lori Hersberger, Michael Hiltbrunner, Dòra Kapusta, Tobias Kaspar, Valeria Stefané-Klausmann & Rainer Klausmann, Mona Knecht, Kueng Caputo, Max Küng, Antonia Kuhn Tischhauser, Mechthild Kunath, Sandra König & Caspar Hoesch, Steffen & Annabelle Lemmerzahl, Mireille Lier, Lutz & Guggisberg, Michael Lütscher, Peter Märkli, Bruno Maurer, Eliette McCouch, Mickry 3, Regula Müdesbacher, Thomas Müllenbach, Peter Münger, Brigit Naef, Jean-Luc Nicollier, René Peier, Marina Porobic, Walter Pfeiffer, David Renggli, Alex Ritter, Remo Roth, Katja Schenker, Marc Scherrer, Klaudia Schifferle, Grazia & Christoph Schifferli, Lena Schliep, Ywan Schumacher, Shirana Shabazi, Sabina Speich, Loredana Sperini, Willy Spiller, Jules Spinatsch, Astrid Staufer, Hugo Stüdeli, Michael Umbricht, Andreas Vogel, Markus Weggenmann, Bettina Zimmermann, Mara Züst, Regula Zwicky.

And to Pietro Mattioli: Without his great commitment to the Painters and Sculptors Building Cooperative Zurich, to the development of its archive with documents and photographs on history and to the cooperative members, this book would not have been possible.

Editor	Painters and Sculptors Building Cooperative Zurich
Idea	Pietro Mattioli
Concept	Luigi Archetti, Stefan Burger, William Lutz, Pietro Mattioli, Valeria Stefané-Klausmann
Photo Editing	Pietro Mattioli, Teo Schifferli
Coordination	Nadine Olonetzky
Texts	Stefan Burger, Adam Jasper, Caroline Kesser, Pietro Mattioli (captions), Bruno Maurer, Burkhard Meltzer, Gabrielle Schaad, Stefan Zweifel
Translation	Catherine Schelbert
Copy editing	Charlotte Eckler
Proofreading	Louise Stein
Design	Teo Schifferli
Lithograph	DZA Druckerei zu Altenburg, Thüringen
Printing and Binding	DZA Druckerei zu Altenburg, Thüringen

© 2021 Verlag Scheidegger & Spiess AG, Zurich
© for the texts the authors
© for the images see photo credit

Verlag Scheidegger & Spiess AG
Niederdorfstrasse 54
8001 Zurich
Switzerland
www.scheidegger-spiess.ch

ISBN 978-3-03942-031-5

All rights reserved; no part of this publication may be reproduced, stored in a retrieval system or transmitted in any form or by any means, electronic, mechanical, photocopying, recording or otherwise, without the prior written consent of the publisher.

Scheidegger & Spiess is being supported by the Federal Office of Culture with a general subsidy for the years 2021–2024.